Gathering the Fragments of Myself

Gathering the Fragments of Myself

A Later-in-Life Coming-of-Age Story of One Woman's Road to Wholeness

by

Jan Banaszek

IVAR HOUSE PUBLISHING

Published 2016

ISBN: 978-0-9975553-1-8
Library of Congress Control Number: 2016912673

Editing and book design by Stacey Aaronson

Published by
Ivar House Press
Los Angeles, CA

Printed in the United States of America

I dedicate this book to my family,
who have been my greatest teachers.

Peggy & Johnny
(Mom & Dad, who were married for 73 years)

Rob, Eileen, Paul,
Sue, Mark, Jill,
Chris, Tracie Lynn,
Luke, and Matthew

PROLOGUE

❧

*H*E DIDN'T MEAN IT.

It was 1949. He had recently returned from World War II and he was edgy. He was wounded in the Battle of the Bulge, living with shrapnel in his body and unresolved, underground feelings that would haunt him for the rest of his life. PTSD was not a familiar concept yet.

Something set him off that particular day.

I was just a baby, enjoying my new environment from the perspective of openness, wonder, and curiosity. I pulled myself up with the help of the coffee table and wobbled back and forth until I got my balance. Reaching for something shiny that was just beyond my reach, I lost my balance and toppled back.

I heard his loud voice above all the others in the room and felt his energy move toward me, like a forceful gust.

He picked me up and threw me against the wall.

SLAM.

I hit the floor, the wind knocked out of me. When I got my breath back and found myself in Mom's arms, she was assuring me that I was going to be okay.

But was I?

1

A SHADOWY CHILDHOOD

S FAR BACK AS I CAN REMEMBER, MY FATHER'S volatile moods permeated our household. His behavior was often unpredictable, and even as a toddler, I recall living in fear. I have a photograph of myself just shy of three, sporting red overalls and a distinct black eye, which Mom says I got when I fell from Dad's arms. Unlike being thrown against the wall, which was an innate body memory that was confirmed by my aunt who witnessed it, I clearly remember that day with Dad ...

I was playing in front of our house on the grass, and I reached out to a butterfly fluttering just beyond my reach. Mom called out to my father. "Look at Jan! Johnny, grab the camera! Hurry!"

But Dad ignored the camera and instead swept me up in his arms, swinging me high in the air. The abruptness of this playful move startled me, but as he tossed me upward, for a moment, I savored the wind on my cheeks and the blissful feeling of falling.

Then, I pushed against his chest, wanting to be put down.

Suddenly I was falling ... falling ... and time stood still.

In that place of stillness, I heard a voice coming from somewhere within me. *"It's okay, Jan. I'm here. You're going to be fine."*

The next thing I remember, I was gasping for breath. I had hit the ground hard, and Mom rushed over to me. I could sense her concern for me, as well as her anger toward Dad.

I will never know what caused him to let me fall that way; in my heart, I know it was an accident. And yet, instinctively, I didn't trust him or feel safe with him, and this fear resonated with me for years to come.

DAD WAS A PASSIONATE MAN WITH A HEART THAT BROKE easily, but that heart was encased in a tough exterior that masked his gentle nature. He was afraid of his own emotions, and while I believe he did his best to keep a lid on them, he always seemed to walk a fine line between calm and eruption. Trying his hardest to make everything in his environment perfect, including his children, he believed that God would provide for him and for us as long as he did "what he was supposed to do." As such, he carefully planned and controlled each day so that nothing would go wrong in his world.

It was a difficult bargain for a man who understood so little about human frailties.

For the first four years of my life, I was the baby of our large family. My brother Rob was the oldest; my sister Eileen was next. I was the third, eventually followed by Paul, Sue, Mark, Jill, Chris, Lynn, Luke, and Matthew.

When my brother Paul arrived, he stole the show. *What's going on?* I wondered. *Did I do something wrong?* I was accustomed to being the cute one, the baby. But despite feeling suddenly abandoned by my parents, wanting to push the intruder away, I couldn't help but love Paul, whom I found undeniably cute and innocent. Eventually, he came to remind me of that place of innocence where all babies should live, that place that for me seemed to have already dissipated.

AS I GREW, THE PROSPECT OF GOING TO SCHOOL AND BEING away from home excited me to the point of a burning desire. At some point I asked my mother when that day would come.

Busy with her housework and keeping an eye on Paul, who was just beginning to walk, she glanced down at me. "Not until you're six, Jan."

"When will I be six? And why do I have to wait 'til I'm six?"

"You're sick?" Distracted by Paul's demands and her favorite soap opera, she had misunderstood me. "I hope you're not sick, but here, let me feel your head."

"No, Mom," I whined. "When will I be six, so I can go to school? Can't I go to school before I'm six?"

I knew about kindergarten, but I wasn't allowed to go. The Catholic school didn't have one, or maybe it was too expensive, and my parents didn't want me to go to a public school.

What's "public"? I wondered. *Is it a different religion?*

But other things were clearly more important in our household than my attending school, so all I could do was push away my feelings and wait.

When the big day arrived, in the fall of 1953, I giddily walked to school with my older sister Eileen, carrying my carefully prepared lunch of bologna sandwich, cookie, and apple in a brown paper bag with my name on it. But when I got there, I noticed right away that the other kids didn't have paper bags—they had shiny new lunchboxes with colorful pictures of cartoon and movie characters.

When I came home that first day, I begged my parents for a lunchbox like that.

"I'm sorry, Jan," Mom said. "We can't afford it."

So despite wanting to have what the other kids had, I accepted that we must be poor and that I would never get a lunchbox, just a special paper bag with my name on it that Mom prepared with love for me every day.

Then one day when I was seven, Dad showed up with a lunchbox for me. It wasn't shiny and new; it was used and resembled what construction workers carried. But it was better than a paper bag, and it was all mine.

The next day, on my way to school with Eileen, I couldn't take my eyes off my "new" lunchbox. Although I wished it were shiny and red, I felt just like the other kids, proud even. Eileen grew impatient as I lagged behind.

"Jan, come on! We have to get to school or we'll be late."

I followed her across the street as if in a trance, clutching my lunchbox tightly, my little feet running to catch up. Then Eileen seemed to run faster and I heard her shout something, but I couldn't understand her words.

At that moment, I felt myself falling. I couldn't comprehend what was happening, but I heard that comforting voice again telling me I was going to be all right, the one that seemed to come from somewhere inside me.

The pavement came up quickly and hit me hard. Everything was out of focus and I couldn't catch my balance or control my body. *Where am I?* I wondered. *What's happening? Where's my lunchbox?*

The next thing I knew, I was lying on the ground by the gutter and people were looking down at me, asking if I was okay. I could hear their concerned voices, but their faces were blurry and unrecognizable. Someone pointed out that my legs were bleeding and told me not to move. When I heard the siren in the distance, I began to cry. In the meantime, Eileen ran back to the house to get Mom.

The man who hit me with his car stayed with me until the ambulance arrived. When Mom came running up the street with Paul holding her hand and baby Sue in her arms, she was devastated that she might lose her little girl. She bent down and loved me the way mothers do, with her soothing voice and soft hands, telling me to let the firemen take care of me and that she would see me soon.

Eileen, tending to the little ones and carrying a burden way too big for a ten-year-old, explained to Mom what happened. "I'm sorry, Mom," she sobbed. "I saw the car, and I told Jan to run with me ... but I guess she didn't hear me."

The firemen laid me on a stretcher and loaded me through double doors. I remember thinking, *Wow! I'm riding in an ambulance. This is fun. Who are these nice men? Where's my lunchbox? Where's Eileen? Where's Mom? I have to go to school.*

The truth was, I was in shock. And in the distance, a place just out of reach, I heard the comforting voice again. It wasn't what was said so much as the tone, almost like the purring of a cat.

"I love you, sweetheart."

I must have passed out then because when I woke up, I was in the emergency room and my leg was hurting. As a doctor wrapped a bandage around my leg, a nurse stroked my forehead and said, "You're going to be okay, Jan. Your dad is on his way in and you're going home."

My heart jumped a beat as I anticipated how angry he would be at me when he arrived.

Shortly after, I heard the familiar sound of Dad clearing his throat. My heart jumped again as I opened my eyes and saw him standing over me. But when he asked me if I was okay, his voice broke, as if he were about to cry.

"Where's my lunchbox?" I asked.

"Don't worry about anything, Jan. Let's go home."

He's being awfully nice to me, I thought. But I couldn't help but worry I had done something wrong and might have to pay for it later.

When I got home, Mom fixed up the couch like a comfy bed for me, turned on the TV, and brought me soup and crackers. For a while, it seemed like everything might just be okay after all.

DESPITE THE FACT THAT EVERYONE KNEW IT WAS AN accident, the man who hit me with his car was quite distraught over it. He came over the next day to see how I was doing, and before he left, he asked my parents if there was anything he could do to help. Mom told him about my lunchbox being crushed, and the man gave them money enough to buy me a new one. Believe it or not, that was all they asked for, and that was all they took.

But I never got a new lunchbox.

I thought about praying for one, but what good would it do? My parents made it clear that even with the man's money, they couldn't afford it, that they needed the money for food.

Around that time I began to wonder in earnest about God—where He was, if He was watching over me, if I really had a guardian angel like they told me in school. *And what about the nice voice that keeps telling me I'm going to be okay?* I pondered. *Who is that?*

That first year, they gave us a catechism in school and told us to memorize it. It was a question-and-answer book about God and the Catholic Church—"the one true church." Although I memorized every word perfectly and was able to answer each question when asked, I didn't feel any closer to what they called God. He was supposedly all knowing, all powerful, the king of creation, and all that, but who was He really?

I asked myself all kinds of questions: Why can't I feel Him? Can He see me doing everything? Why can't He stop Dad from being so mean?

While bringing me a lunchbox when I wanted one so desperately and we couldn't afford one was an act of generosity on Dad's part, it was an unusual one for him. It would have been more like him to become angry. Why he wasn't that time, I'll never know.

That shortly treasured lunchbox became a symbol of things longed for and received, only to one day be taken away.

DAD WAS A STRICT CATHOLIC. MOM FOLLOWED SUIT TO keep the peace, and the rest of us didn't have a choice. We had to go to church, no matter how we were feeling, and we had to pretend we were happy. Dad would march us up to the front of the church on Sundays to show everyone just what a perfect family we were. He also somehow managed to control his temper in church, making him look like the perfect father. After we took our seats, though, Dad would often nod in and out of consciousness, struggling to stay awake.

Church was so quiet and serious that I sometimes felt compelled to laugh out loud. It wasn't that I was irreverent; it was simply that some things were hysterical to me, like the woman in front of us with the feather in her hat that moved in funny directions, or the long, deep growl of someone's stomach during a moment of silence. I did my best to stifle my laughter, though, despite how difficult it was; I knew if Dad heard me laughing during something so important to him, I would cause him embarrassment and create a crack in the image of our ideal family.

I'm sorry, God, I would say, *but how can you expect me to be still when I'm so full of life?*

To me, God was like Dad. Distant, controlling, powerful, and scary.

NEW BABIES ARRIVED IN OUR FAMILY EVERY COUPLE OF years, and I was always overwhelmed when Mom brought one home, not only because I was filled with the unblemished energy they carried, but also because it meant another child Eileen and I had to care for.

While we adored our siblings, being the two oldest girls, Eileen and I felt responsible to help our mother with them in every way we could. She didn't demand it, but I, especially, saw how she struggled with so many babies to tend to and automatically took on the role of "second mother." As Eileen was older than me by three years, I leaned on her to take on the responsibility while I helped. I followed her commands as she tried to keep things in order so Dad wouldn't blow up.

Whenever I heard sounds from the new baby's bedroom, I'd be there, finding the little one standing against the edge of the crib, jumping up and down, hands outstretched. If I went to a friend's house or an activity after school, I felt guilty for being away and worried about each of them.

When dinnertime approached, Eileen and I would clean up everyone and hustle them to the table. We had to ensure that all of us were quiet and in our places when Dad walked in after a frustrating day at a job he didn't like.

At the sound of the tires rolling over the loose gravel in the driveway, my body would tighten up. "Dad's home!" I'd yell. Mom would be cooking dinner, keeping an eye on the newest baby in the house, as Eileen ran in to help.

As soon as Dad walked in, the energy would shift immediately as we all froze in our places. He would sometimes walk into the kitchen, his face tense and tight, his body smelling of sweat, as he sidled over to Mom and tried to hug and kiss her passionately.

She would push him away, saying, "Johnny, not now."

Peering through the doorway, I would wince at the rejection, watching for the telltale sign that he was about to explode. When he bit down on his lower lip, we knew all hell was about to break loose. I would pray while holding my breath not to see his teeth bare down on his lip.

BY THE TIME I WAS TEN, I HAD FOUR YOUNGER SIB-lings—all of whom I believed I had the responsibility to protect. Without Eileen—my rock, anchor, and mentor—to share secret laughter and all the mothering responsibilities with, my childhood wouldn't have been the same. It wasn't all bad—don't get me wrong. We did go on some vacations as a family and had fun sightseeing, hiking, and exploring new places, but I simply couldn't imagine any of it without Eileen's presence.

Despite the arrival of new grandchildren on a regular basis, however, we rarely saw our grandparents. Dad's relatives lived in New York and Mom's, including her own mother, didn't visit much. Grandma didn't like Dad, so she simply stayed away; she hadn't wanted Mom to marry him in the first place. Every time Mom got pregnant, she was afraid to tell Grandma because she knew her mother wouldn't approve.

Grandma was so detached from us that I remember one rare visit with her when she asked Eileen in a soft, yet distant voice, her breath like stale smoke, if "her friend would like something to drink." She hadn't recognized me. I recall the sensation at that moment of sinking deeper into my body, feeling invisible and sad that my own grandmother didn't even know me.

But on those few occasions when Dad's relatives came to visit—especially his sister, Aunt Lil, who was strong, feisty, and socially savvy—it was a treat. Aunt Lil knew how to dress: stylish suits, the back seams of her hose perfectly straight, matching high heels to round out the ensemble. Her hair was fashionably gray and curly, and unlike Mom, she was tall and commanded attention. When I looked up at her, I saw her bright red lips speak with confidence, never holding back what she was thinking.

One time she looked at me and said to my parents, "Now that one's a heartbreaker. She's going to have them lining up at the door to go out with her."

I immediately took what she said and visualized boys lined up at the door, without my having to do anything but simply stand there being cute. I had no idea that I might have to actually do something to make this happen. Unfortunately, I wasn't learning from Mom how to dress with any degree of fashion sense; we were lucky if we got one new outfit a year. What's more, there was never a line of boys at the door, at least not for me.

MY BROTHER ROB WAS MY SENIOR BY SIX YEARS, AND I adored him. A quiet and elusive boy, he was also inexplicably charismatic. His friends swarmed around him like he was a king. I wondered what it was that drew people to him, what I'd have to do to be like Rob or to be with someone like him.

Rob's friends would come over to hang out with him and sometimes help him with the old blue car he worked on in the yard, but that was not their only reason for being there. Strangely enough, they liked being at our house. I would overhear them talking about the girls they liked and how they could get what they wanted from them. When they were finished working on the car, Rob and his friends would come in the house all greasy and laughing.

One time, Rob's friend Dennis said to me, "Hey, Jan, did you get a haircut? It looks really cute."

My face flushed and my stomach went queasy. "Thank you," I said and looked down.

This was the first compliment I recalled receiving from a boy, and it made me wonder if they were finally going to start lining up at the door like Aunt Lil said. For a moment, my heart leapt with excitement, but it was immediately eclipsed by fear.

One evening when I was twelve, I walked out of the bathroom after my shower, wearing a sheer summer nightie with my hair still wet. Dad stared at me from across the room, and something about the way he looked at me caused me to quickly put my head down and pretend I didn't see him. Shame and anger flooded my being as I wondered, What does he want? Is he going to hug me too tight again?

The little kids were already in bed and Eileen was doing her homework. I put the TV on and sat down on the living room floor. Dad had gone into the kitchen, but I knew that at any moment he might come in and get angry with me, telling me I was wasting my time and to do something productive. When he didn't, I escaped into one of my favorite TV shows, one with a happy family where the kids could make mistakes that were solvable, and the parents always forgave them by the end of the show.

Afterward, I went into the kitchen and there he was with Mom.

"You look like your mother when she was young, so pretty," he said, his eyes squinting inappropriately.

Blood rushed to my face, and I felt like I needed to shower all over again to rid my body of him, as if he had seeped into me somehow. The last time he had hugged me, I had felt for a moment like I couldn't breathe, like he was stealing my soul.

I looked at Mom, but she merely giggled demurely and looked away.

Mom often invited Rob's friends to have dinner with us. Though I was never comfortable inviting my friends to our house, I was relieved when Rob's buddies agreed to stay—we were able to breathe easier those nights because we all knew that Dad would be on his best behavior in front of the boys. It was like he was a different person when other people were around—no tense glares around the table if one of us wasn't eating quietly enough, no outbursts if someone spilled a glass of milk or said something he didn't like. We were more like a TV family.

One night, Dennis came for dinner, and I had to constantly look down at my plate to hide that my face was flushed and hot. When I did catch his glance, I retreated quickly back into myself. And it wasn't that I was afraid of my father catching a glimpse of my coyness. It was that all I could think was how I wanted this boy to like me, yet stay as far away from me as possible.

Although my father adored my mother, I watched her all throughout their marriage be at his beck and call, always tending to his every need, afraid to turn him down or to say no. If Dad didn't get what he wanted, Mom would warn us to be careful because "Daddy was in a bad mood." As we got older, we came to understand that if Daddy didn't get sex, he could be mean. Though she didn't tell us outright, somehow we knew merely by the way Mom talked about it, as if it were an obligation she failed to perform and we all had to live with the consequences.

IN 1962, EILEEN ANNOUNCED THAT SHE WAS GOING TO enter the convent. She was seventeen, I was fourteen, and her news felt like someone had just removed one of my organs. She was so much a part of me, of the glue that held the family together. I immediately felt the heaviness of the responsibility for caring for our six younger siblings fall on me and wondered how I would ever manage without her.

I tried to will her to stay but only to myself, afraid to say something outward that would get in the way of her plans. I kept hoping something would stop her, but she was determined—it was her way out.

I found myself blaming God for taking her away from me. The quiet, comforting voice was there but far away, eclipsed by other louder voices telling me that I wasn't good enough, that I wasn't safe, that I was trapped. But when we all piled into the station wagon and Dad drove us ninety miles from Los Angeles to deliver Eileen to her new home, a retreat center in the Santa Barbara Mountains, I was overwhelmed by the beautiful, magical place where young women in white dedicated themselves to God.

Is this where you are, God? I asked. *Is this what I need to do to find you?*

Back at home I tried hard to appear normal, but I was falling apart inside. I gulped down the pain and accompanying nausea over and over, until finally I couldn't take it anymore and threw up all over my desk one day in class. Someone took me to the bathroom and helped me clean up, but later I overheard some of the girls talking about it, making fun of me. I was mortified that I hadn't been able to keep my body under control.

I begged Mom to take me to the doctor, telling her that I

hurt really bad and didn't know what was wrong with me. Although we didn't go to the doctor in those days unless it was an emergency, Mom and Dad took me in. The doctor kept me in the hospital overnight and ran some tests, but they found nothing physically wrong with me. Still, I felt better lying in the hospital bed where I felt safe and nice people were taking care of me.

The next morning the doctor came in and sat on my bed.

"Jan, honey," she said in a gentle voice, "Your problem is peer pressure. You're trying too hard to be like your sister, and it's too much for you. You're not her. You're you."

I looked away; her words touched me deeply, cutting through the mask I had been living behind. It was the first time anyone had recognized my irrational desire to imitate Eileen. It was also the first time anyone had told me it was all right to be me.

ALTHOUGH THE PAIN WENT AWAY EVENTUALLY, I WAS plagued with headaches and occasional stomach pain well into my adult life. That kind doctor had given me permission to be myself, but what no one, including me, understood was that I was a long way from knowing how to accomplish that seemingly simple life task, that I was miles and years away from that most vital of endeavors called learning to love and respect myself.

2

THE LAST VIRGIN

FTER HIGH SCHOOL, AFRAID TO MAKE TOO BIG A move, I continued living at home and attended the Catholic college up the hill from the high school for two years. I strove to discover myself amid the never-ending chaos that subsided a bit as my younger siblings grew up, but after two years, I finally had enough and felt the strong pull to get out of there—it was time to find my identity in the world outside my family and the Catholic Church.

I worked hard in my uncle's office for a few months to earn enough money, and for my third year of college, I transferred to a university an hour away in Orange County, moving out of my parents' home and into the dorms to experience college life.

One afternoon, hanging out in the dorm with several of the girls, the conversation turned to stories about boys, wild parties, and getting "plastered." One girl in particular, Diana, whom I had known from Catholic school, suddenly spoke up. In a clear voice that everyone could hear, she said, "Any virgins in the room?"

I froze. I felt that every eye was on me, as if they all knew I had never been to a wild party or even dated a boy.

Diana was smart and conservative, having grown up in one of those rich homes where I imagined everyone got what they needed and wanted. I noticed that every weekend she would pack a bag and stay with her boyfriend, and I couldn't help but wonder if she was having sex with him. *I thought we weren't supposed to do that until we got married*, my Catholic upbringing admonished.

"Let's take a poll," said Diana, a devilish gleam in her eye. "Write 'yes' or 'no' on a slip of paper. You don't have to put your name on it."

The room filled with giggles as we passed a sheet of paper around and tore off little pieces to pass to Diana. I wrote my answer quickly and passed it on.

"Oooooh!" she squealed. "One of us is still a virgin."

Blood rushed to my face. I desperately wanted to make myself invisible like I was used to doing at home. It would have been a good time for the floor to open up and swallow me. I laughed nervously as I internally collapsed into myself.

I assumed that as the girls started laughing it was about me, but then the conversation shifted as the dinner bell sounded. We all headed for the cafeteria, which was always a treat for me because, unlike at home, I could eat whatever I wanted and didn't have to share or eat sparingly so everyone else at the table would have enough.

That night, I had a dream. In it I was falling, out of control, past objects and flashes of lights and people I didn't recognize hiding in caves. Then I landed near a cave. As I approached it, I saw a light in the distance and a figure walking toward me carrying a lantern. I stepped back. The figure, a man, I think, walked steadily toward me. I glanced behind myself and realized I was trapped; if I backed up one more step, I would fall back into an abyss. He was getting closer and I could sense the edge behind me. Then suddenly, he dropped the lantern and it fell to the ground with a crashing sound.

I woke up abruptly, and my consciousness shifted to the present as my roommate came home from a date.

"Hi, Jan," Sandy said. "You awake?"

"Yeah," I answered, not wanting to chat but deciding to share. "I was having a weird dream."

"Another weird dream? What about?"

I was about to tell her when she flipped on the light and began undressing, humming a familiar song that I knew I wouldn't be able to get out of my head. There was no point in telling her about my dream. She was in her own world.

"So how was your date?" I asked, now wide awake, trying to be polite. I stilled my breath to appear calm, but inside I was crumbling with jealousy. Maybe it would be different this time. Maybe this guy hadn't fallen under her spell.

"It was incredible," she began. "I think I'm in love again. This guy is so perfect. He's tall, gorgeous, funny, and so smart. I think he's the one."

Yeah, right, I thought, *I'm sure she'll find something wrong with him.*

"What about David?" I asked.

"What about him?

"You said you were in love with him too."

"So what? He blew it. Time to move on."

She was devastated when she broke up with David—I had sat and listened and comforted her for hours. Now she was moving on, just like that? I saw the ugly pattern forming between us: I was repeatedly there for her when she was in crisis; then, just when I was feeling closer to her, she rebounded into another relationship or developed a new interest, ignoring me until the next time she needed me. It angered and confused me—I didn't like being used when convenient, but I allowed myself to be that person anyway.

"So what if this new guy does the same thing?" I pushed,

hoping she'd see that our friendship was more important than some new guy she just met. "Shouldn't you take your time and make sure he's trustworthy?"

"No, Jan, you don't get it. This guy's different. He's wonderful. He would never hurt me."

I felt resentment flare inside me as I imagined never having a decent date, Sandy never having to worry about being alone.

Though I was envious in the moment, however, Sandy fascinated me. She seemed wild, like an untamed horse. She wasn't afraid to speak her mind. She was fun. And she was sexy. I'd always been much too conservative, too well behaved. It wasn't that I didn't want to let go and be wild, but it just didn't come naturally to me.

I watched as she removed one piece of clothing at a time, admiring herself in the mirror, still humming that silly song. I held the covers close to me over my flannel nightie.

"Jan, there's a party tomorrow night in Newport Beach. Let's go."

"What kind of party?" I asked, my tone betraying my apprehension. "And what about your new boyfriend?"

"He has to study. It's just a party—I'm sure some cute guys will be there. Some of the other girls are going. It'll be fun. You might even meet someone."

Fat chance, I thought. If I did meet anyone it was usually the clingy guys. They would hang around me all night and I wouldn't know how to get rid of them. And with Sandy there, I wouldn't have a chance. Guys wouldn't even notice me.

"I don't know. I don't think so," I said.

"You'll never meet anyone if you don't get out."

I looked away without responding. As much as I didn't want to admit it, I figured she was right.

"You can't expect them to just knock on your door. You have to get out there," she added.

I guess she didn't have someone like Aunt Lil who told her differently. How could my clever, stylish aunt have been wrong?

She persisted. "Stop being so resistant, Jan."

"Okay," I finally said. I knew she wasn't going to let up on me. "What should I wear?"

"Let's go out tomorrow after class and get you something sexy."

Sexy? What was the point of that? I wasn't sexy. I would have preferred to wear my old jeans and a sweatshirt.

"All right," I said, giving in.

"Don't worry. We'll find you the perfect outfit."

Easy for you to say, I retorted with my eyes.

THE NEXT NIGHT THE DORM WAS ABUZZ WITH GIRLS getting ready for the party. They ran from one room to another, sharing makeup, playing loud music, and singing. I wished I could get in the mood, but this scenario was a completely foreign one to me. My body felt tight and uncomfortable as I put on my black tights with the short skirt and lacy see-through blouse I had bought that afternoon.

As I looked in the mirror, I wondered what would it be like to feel good about my body. I imagined myself standing on a corner on Sunset Boulevard in fishnet stockings and knee-high boots, my hair wild, wearing lots of makeup, proud of my body, ready for action, guys eyeing me with desire.

But just as abruptly, I thought, *That's not me. Those girls are bad.* Only they seemed so confident and free. And I was the only virgin in the room.

"You look great, Jan," Sandy said, blowing in.

"Oh," I said, startled out of my daze. "Thanks."

"Wow! What a knockout," said one of the other girls. "You should dress like that all the time, Jan."

"Thank you," I said quietly as I felt my cheeks flush.

Despite what seemed to be genuine compliments, I couldn't help but feel out of place, alone even. Suddenly, I sensed the voice again coming from somewhere inside of me, soft and gentle.

"Jan, I love you."

3

JOEL

O N THE WAY TO THE PARTY IN NEWPORT BEACH, THE girls coached me on what to expect.

"Watch out for Joel," one of them said. "He'll probably be there again. He's such a flirt. Charming, but dangerous. He asked me out last week, and then when he came to pick me up, he hit on my roommate."

I rolled my eyes in the dark of the back seat, wondering who would ever want to be with a guy like that.

The party was already in full swing when we arrived. Sandy was her usual boisterous self, joining the party as if she had already been there for hours. The other girls started mingling. As I drifted around looking for a safe place to land, I felt as if my dark cloud of insecurity would engulf me.

"Hi," I said to someone I didn't know, trying to reach out. No response. *I must not have said it loudly enough.* So I poured myself a soda and found a spot on the couch. The music was blaring; people were dancing and drinking and talking in small groups. I saw a balcony door open and caught a glimpse of a couple making out.

Then I spotted a guy dancing with several girls. Boy, was he cute, and obviously full of himself, gyrating like he was God's gift to women. The way he was acting reminded me of my father. But I couldn't keep myself from staring—he was so sexy and he moved perfectly with the music. His curly brown hair, moustache, and a cigarette dangling from his lip completed the look of total coolness. I glanced at the girls who were around him, and a lot of them were clearly charmed.

I was mesmerized by him when in the middle of a song, he made eye contact with me. I thought to look around to see if I was mistaken, but then he left his entourage and strutted over to me. He pulled me off the couch so fast that I didn't have time to say no. The next thing I knew I was in the center of the room, my heart pounding, grooving with this guy as people watched us. Adrenaline shot through my body; my legs went weak. I hung on for dear life as he swirled me around and around until I was dizzy. But in the midst of the chaos, I noticed that his hands were warm, his smile contagious, his eyes bright blue and sparkly. And through the blur I couldn't help but see the other girls looking at me. He caught my eye and winked.

A slow song came on, and he pulled me close to him. His mouth was next to my ear, and I could hear him breathing. His breath was warm and comforting, and I began breathing in rhythm with him. Butterflies danced in my stomach as his hands began to roam toward my butt. I wondered if I should stop him, pull back, or slap him. Only it felt kind of good so I did nothing.

When the song ended, I surrendered as he dipped me. Then, taking my hand, he walked me out to the balcony. My body was shaking, partly from the cold and partly from the emotions welling up inside me, while my mind was busy with thoughts. *Maybe he's it. Maybe he's the one I'll fall in love with and live happily ever after.*

"I'm Joel," he said.

Joel? Oh great. So much for the "happily ever after" idea.

"Hi. I'm Jan."

"Would you like something to drink?"

"Yes. Thank you. A soda, please."

I held my breath and then sighed deeply as he walked away with a bounce in his step. No wonder girls fell for him— he was cute, and sexy. The spicy scent of his cologne lingered in the air as I decided he must think I'm better than the other girls.

Maybe he's not a big flirt like they think. Maybe there's more to him than they know.

Joel came back carrying a beer in one hand, my soda in the other, with his jacket over his shoulder. He handed me my drink, then he put his jacket around me. His bright blue eyes looked mischievous, like he had a secret. He gazed intently at me and I was mesmerized again.

"You have the most beautiful eyes I've ever seen," he said.

Was it a pick-up line? Possibly. But I was flattered. I felt my body drawn toward him like a magnet as he leaned in closer. I put my head on his chest. He hugged me tight, and I melted into his body as if we were one. I allowed myself to lose all sense of where I was. Then he leaned down and kissed me.

Initially I pushed him away, afraid he would find out I didn't know how to kiss. But when he leaned in again, his lips felt warm and moist. He pushed his tongue gently past my lips, moving slowly and deliberately.

Though it felt heavenly, I couldn't help but question the energy coursing through my body, fearful that I might lose control, that he might take advantage of me.

He pulled away slowly. "Wow! Nice," he said.

I smiled, hopeful he really meant it.

We hung out the rest of the evening, and then after the party, Joel asked Sandy if he could ride back to the dorm with us, that he'd get a ride home later. Since the other girls had left with someone else, Joel and I had the back seat of Sandy's car all to ourselves. I was cold, and he put his arm around me and hugged me close. I felt as if we'd been together for a long time, yet the sparks that passed between us kept reminding me that this was all new and unfamiliar.

Sandy dropped us off at the dorm, saying she was going to see her boyfriend. I doubted I'd see her for the rest of the weekend as Joel offered to walk me up to my room. Restrictions about late-night guests at the dorm were pretty lax, so I accepted.

"I just want to hold you for a while, Jan," he said. "Can I come in?"

"I'd like that," I said.

I don't know why, but I trusted Joel. I wanted to be close to him, in his arms.

We walked into the room and lay down on my bed. Suddenly all I could think was, *Why did I leave my clothes on the floor? I hope he doesn't notice the dust on my desk. I wasn't expecting company.*

But Joel didn't seem to notice. He appeared completely taken with me. Even when I confessed that I had never kissed anyone before, he was sweet about it.

"You're doing great," he said. "I'll be happy to teach you more."

True to his word, Joel was an excellent teacher. I got lost in his kissing lessons, feeling myself going in and out of ecstasy, sure of my limit but unsure where we were going. We eventually fell asleep in each other's arms. When we woke up a few hours later, our excitement became even more intense.

Just when I wasn't sure I could harness my feelings anymore, Joel got up abruptly, saying he had to leave. I sensed that was his way of controlling himself and respecting me, which made me feel even more drawn to him.

"I'll call you," he promised. Then, as he closed the door, he whispered, "You're a great kisser."

I smiled and waved good-bye, then fell back onto the bed in a whoosh.

At last I was feeling what people had been talking about, what I'd seen in the movies. I'd had crushes before, but always from a distance. No one had ever responded to me this way before. I wanted him to come back. I wanted more, and I wanted it *now*.

But I was worried too.

The girls warned me he was a flirt. What if he didn't come back? What if he treated me like all the other girls he'd kissed and never called?

TO MY RELIEF, JOEL CALLED A FEW DAYS LATER. HE ASKED me out to a movie on Saturday night, and of course I said yes. I couldn't wait. All I wanted was to be with him again.

Joel said he would pick me up at 7:00, and I agonized all day over what to wear on the date. I didn't want to dress too sexy, but I did want to be attractive and feel grown up. As usual, I opted for comfort, so I put on a pair of black pants and a light blue sweater. It was a cold night, so I wore my black boots and draped my brown pea coat by my purse. I wore just enough makeup and a light lipstick. I knew it would come off anyway, the thought of which made me tingle all over.

I was ready right on time. Sandy had already left for her date, so I walked back and forth, poking again through my closet to see if I could find something better to wear. I looked in the mirror multiple times to make sure everything was in place. I peeked outside; I opened the door several times to see if he might be standing there. The feeling of butterflies in my stomach was overwhelming.

This must be it, I thought, *I must be in love.* Then, *What if it doesn't work out? What if I get pregnant?*

There were so many things to consider. I still believed in saving myself for marriage, but how long could I hold out?

At around 7:30, I heard Joel's voice in the hallway. He said hi to one of my dorm mates in a way that seemed like he knew her. But it didn't matter. He was coming to see *me.*

Joel held my hand through the entire movie, and every time he put pressure on my fingers, or in the palm of my hand, energy surged through me like an electric current. I felt like I was on fire the entire time.

Afterward, Joel drove me to a restaurant for a late dinner. Every time we came to a stoplight, he would lean over and kiss me gently. I grew to love red lights. During the meal, I had to force myself to eat, as love devoured my appetite.

After dinner we kissed for quite some time in his car, but then once again, he showed himself to be a gentleman and took me back to the dorm. He promised to call, and he did.

ON OUR SECOND DATE, JOEL ASKED IF I MINDED IF WE stopped at his parents' house and I said that was fine, though I was nervous about meeting them, wondering if they would like me. He told me he had an older sister with three kids, as well as six younger siblings who were still at home. I was comforted that he came from a big family too and tried to re-member everyone's names while we drove toward the house. After we parked, Joel opened my door and took my hand. As we neared the house, though, he let go and burst through the door ahead of me.

His father sat on the far side of the couch, a big grin on his face. He looked me up and down, winked, and said, "Well, she's a pretty one."

Joel's mom was sitting on the other end of the couch, her feet propped up in her husband's lap, as he gave her a foot massage. She didn't say much to me, but instead continued to enjoy the massage as they watched TV. Joel's younger siblings seemed excited to meet me and reminded me of my own family, except they seemed freer, without the familiar tension I always felt in my house.

At one point his younger sister Evelyn came through the front door with her much quieter boyfriend. "I see you're up to no good," she said sarcastically to Joel. Then they went off to the den and closed the door. I couldn't imagine her parents allowing that. I wondered what else they easily condoned.

Joel's mom invited us to have dinner with them the following day. I was surprised when everyone grabbed for food at once—there was plenty to go around, and they talked freely, joking around, making fun of one another. It felt worlds apart from the silent, tense, and fear-laden dinners I was used to at home.

Joel's father had piercing, icy blue eyes, similar to Joel's. He was handsome in his own way, but there was something about the way he looked at me that made me uneasy. I felt like an object being appraised as he said to Joel, clicking his tongue twice from the side of his mouth, "You'd better hang on to this one."

What was it with fathers? Why did they act so inappropriate?

I merely giggled awkwardly, trying to will the blood from rushing to my face. Receiving what seemed to be positive attention was nice, but I could feel my body tightening up and becoming protective, like a good Catholic girl.

AS THE WEEKS WENT BY AND JOEL AND I CONTINUED dating, I not only felt comfortable saying I had a boyfriend, but I was beginning to feel like I was finally "normal" too. Joel gave me every indication that he was as in love with me as I was with him, and I had decided I wouldn't be going back to college the following year. Despite being only one year from graduating, I was longing for a break. I wanted to see the world, have adventures, and find myself. And, of course, I wanted to be with Joel.

Although he had a decent job working for the phone company, Joel's parents and some friends were encouraging him to go to college or he would most likely get drafted. But he wasn't interested in school. And I didn't care if he went to college or not. I was in love and fully believed I was headed to a happily ever after.

ON SUNDAYS, I WENT TO CHURCH WITH A GIRL FROM MY dorm, but it was more out of fear than desire: I went because I didn't want to be condemned to hell.

One Sunday morning after a date with Joel, I woke up late and missed my ride. When Sandy came back later that day and saw me upset, she said, "I think God will forgive you for missing church this time."

I felt guilty, but I couldn't help wondering if maybe it was time to break away from my childhood routine. What was I being faithful to anyway? God? God only made me angry. Whenever I prayed, I received no clear answers. I had tried all my life up to then to be perfect so that God and my father would love me— or maybe so they wouldn't punish me. But the more perfect I tried to be, the more I lost my sense of self.

Not long after that, Sandy and I were discussing her robust romantic life when she abruptly attacked me.

"Jan, who do you think you are?" she snapped. "Stop being so passive and say something. I feel like you're judging me all the time. You need to get a life of your own and stop butting into mine. I'm tired of taking care of you, and I'm tired of walking on eggshells around you. You're too sensitive. And you're such a goody-goody. Why don't you grow up?"

It felt like a slap in the face, and I promptly broke down and cried, saying how sorry I was, though I wasn't sure what I'd done wrong.

I went to see the dorm supervisor in tears, barely able to talk as I babbled on about how badly I had been treated by my roommate. She calmed me down and listened without being critical, but then she suggested that I look at how my behavior may have triggered something in Sandy.

A few days later, I sat down with Sandy and apologized for what I might have done to make her angry. She admitted that my being naïve and still a virgin made her feel like she was behaving like a slut. Turns out, she'd been having sex since she was fourteen and her insecurities got the best of her.

That cleared up a lot for me, but our relationship was never the same afterward. Despite the break in our bond, though, Sandy unknowingly helped me realize how sheltered I was and how little I understood about the effects of my behavior on others. Armed with a fresh perspective, and set on leaving school at the end of the semester, I was ready for my next adventures.

THAT SUMMER, I MOVED BACK INTO MY PARENTS' HOUSE. It wasn't ideal, but I needed time to work and save some money before I could live on my own. Joel often drove the hour or so from Santa Ana to Hollywood to visit me, and my family accepted him readily. Mom was sure I had found my prince, and my younger sisters were delighted with my new boyfriend, hanging around us, flirting, and vying for his attention. Joel smiled and winked at them a lot, maybe enjoying their attention a little too much. He even flirted with Mom, who gave him her demure smile in return.

Every night when Joel brought me home from our date, we would spend hours out on the porch talking and kissing quietly. The chemistry between us was strong and difficult to resist. Everything felt funny and I felt out of control, yet I remained clear with Joel about my boundaries.

Confident I had found my one true love, I introduced Joel to my best friend Christine, whom I had met working at the same department store in Hollywood when I was eighteen. Though we were the same age and both in college, we were nothing alike: Christine and her mom had moved to Hollywood when Christine was sixteen, leaving her alcoholic father behind; she had no siblings and seemed happy about that; and she was much more sophisticated than I was—she dressed in style, her hair was perfectly in place, and she knew about politics. I, on the other hand, still looked like a little girl and lacked her worldly air. Christine was often mistaken for my mom or my aunt when we went out together, which was insulting to us both.

Fortunately, we quickly discovered that we had a sense of humor in common, as well as a sense of adventure. Over the years, despite our differences, life had a quirky way of keeping us together.

One stellar quality Christine possessed was being able to identify red flags in my life that I often wasn't as quick to catch. Although she was sometimes blunt with me about her concerns, she was always looking out for my best interests, even when it didn't feel that way. So I was nervous about introducing Joel to Christine, afraid she wouldn't approve of him or our relationship. Her approval meant a lot to me, so I was doubly hopeful she'd be supportive.

When they met, it seemed to go well. Joel winked at Christine, which to me meant he liked her. But later she told me that she thought he was making a pass at her. I, of course, was clueless. She liked him, she said, but she wanted me to be careful.

Most everyone else, however, approved of our relationship. Joel and I were in love, and it was the most wonderfully delicious sensation I had ever experienced. I wasn't sure what was next for me, but nothing mattered because all I could think about was Joel and the future we would have together.

4

⚜

SEA CHANGE

*I*T WAS 1968. THE VIETNAM WAR WAS IN FULL swing, and controversy and unrest seemed to hang in the air. Protests were popping up, and a lot of people were angry about our involvement.

One evening as Joel drove us to dinner, he was unusually quiet. He reached out and put his hand on my leg, but when we stopped at the traffic signals, he didn't reach over and kiss me like he normally did. Eventually, he took his hand away and began playing with his moustache.

"Is everything okay?" I asked.

"Yes. Everything's fine."

He didn't say much at dinner and I wasn't hungry. I felt guilty for not eating my food, but I knew something was up.

When we left the restaurant and got into the car, he gave me a serious look. "Jan, there's something I need to tell you."

"What? Are you okay?"

He put my hands in his, caressing my fingers.

"Jan, I enlisted in the Army."

I snatched my hands away as my throat went dry and my stomach knotted up. I struggled to hold back tears.

Oh God, I thought, *this can't be happening to me. What if he gets killed and leaves me all alone?*

Finally I said, "Why would you do that? Couldn't you wait to see if they drafted you?"

"It's only a matter of time until they draft me," he said. "I figured I might as well get it over with. I'm not going to school right now and I'm tired of working for the phone company. The Army offered me a good deal. I'm going to be in Communications, so I'll be learning more about what I'm already interested in, and they'll pay me for it. They'll pay for my education too. It doesn't get better than that."

"But what about Vietnam? What if they send you there?"

"That's possible, but it probably won't happen. I'll be stationed somewhere here in the States, most likely."

"Where?"

"I don't know yet. Basic training will be at Fort Ord. You can come with my parents when they drop me off."

"How much time do you have?" I asked, my voice betraying my worry.

"I leave next Friday."

He pulled me close to his chest. As I looked into his eyes and tears ran down my face, I felt my whole life falling apart.

As far back as I could remember, I had felt lost and empty, and this was the love that was supposed to fill me forever. Joel was my savior, and now he was being taken away from me for a stupid war.

"I love you, Kitten," he assured me. "I'm not doing this to hurt you."

Too late, I thought.

There in his arms, my pain and desperation soon gave way to anger. I found myself reasoning, *Fine. Good. I'm glad you're leaving. I was feeling trapped anyway. Isn't there more to life than just you?* Then, *Wait ... Please don't leave me here alone.*

Every time I looked at Joel, my eyes would well with emotion. My heart was breaking open and I had no control over it.

I STAYED WITH JOEL AT HIS FAMILY'S HOME THE NIGHT before he left for boot camp. We cuddled until the wee hours of the morning and then, before anyone else awoke, I crept back into the bed his mother had made up for me and fell asleep.

When I got up a few hours later, Joel was up and getting ready. I looked down the long hallway and caught a glimpse of him in the bathroom, shaving. He was wearing his Army uniform, looking so handsome and ready for his next adventure. That picture stayed with me for a long time.

When we climbed into the family station wagon and his dad turned the key in the ignition, we clung to each other in the back seat. Joel's touch was like magic to me. I was going to miss his smell and his deep sexy voice. But I also realized there were things about him I wouldn't miss. He was full of sarcastic comments and stupid jokes, and he sounded like a giddy schoolgirl when he laughed.

But just when I decided I could live without him and his faults, he winked at me and I lit up again with that tingly feeling in my body. There was no denying it. Joel had become a part of me. He was my safe harbor in an unpredictable world.

AFTER JOEL WAS GONE, I FELT I DIDN'T BELONG AT HOME anymore. And though I had briefly reconsidered it, I decided for certain not to return for my senior year. I still had my job at the department store, but I was adrift, wondering where I should go, what I should be doing, and worrying that Joel might never come back.

I knew there was more to life than having a man, that I needed to get out there and find myself, but inside I was torn.

The thing was, I didn't know who I was outside my relationship with Joel.

I was experiencing the whole world in turmoil. It was also a time of exploring new lifestyles; it wasn't cool anymore to simply get married and have kids, to lead a conventional life. I didn't mind that so much, but if I did choose the traditional path, there was one thing I did know: I didn't want to end up trapped like my mother.

I decided that before Joel got back, perhaps this was my opportunity to see what else was out there for me. At any rate, it was time to get away from the craziness and chaos of home. Little did I know then that I was taking the chaos with me.

AFTER JOEL FINISHED BOOT CAMP, I SAW HIM FOR A FEW weeks. There was an unspoken tension between us, though, and he finally said, "Kitten, I don't know where they're sending me for certain."

He didn't have to say it; I knew in my heart he was going to Vietnam and that I would not see him again for at least a year.

"I'm sorry, Kitten," he continued. "It's possible I'll go to Vietnam. I didn't know there was such a strong chance of me going there when I enlisted."

It didn't matter where he was going; it was far away from me.

"Damn you, Joel," I said. "Why did you have to do this?"

"I promise you, Jan, I will come back to you."

But I knew no one could make a promise like that.

We spent every moment we could together, often driving down to the beach in Santa Monica and cuddling under the stars, listening to the breaking waves. It was an odd reminder that life would go on.

"See that star up there?" he'd say. "When I'm away and I see that star, I'll be thinking of you and how much I love you."

I was comforted by the single star in the vastness of the sky that would keep us together no matter what, but I also knew it was a fantasy. I had my own hopes and dreams, and so did he.

On one of our nights under the stars, he looked into my eyes with that sexy twinkle. "I hope our second child is a girl, with eyes like yours," he said.

"Second child? What about the first one?"

"The first one should be a boy, like me," he said with a grin. "He'll be big and strong, and he'll protect his little sister."

I gave a fake, closed-mouth smile, at once caught up in the dream of being a mother to Joel's children and cringing at the thought of having to care for babies all over again.

Soon after, Joel was deployed.

I WAS TWENTY-ONE YEARS OLD, ALONE, AND MISSING Joel. I was also craving adventure.

In the fall of 1968, I decided to take my aunt up on her offer to come to New York. For years, Dad's sister, Aunt Bertha, had been inviting me to come and stay for an extended visit. The timing felt right to me. I saw this as my big opportunity to begin exploring the world.

Joel wrote often. Each letter displayed the APO San Francisco return address scrawled in his familiar handwriting on the upper left corner of the flimsy blue government envelope. His words were sweet and passionate, but he was living in a different world, one that was far from the freedom I was experiencing.

Hi Kitten,
I miss you so much. I think about you all the time. It's so
lonely here. We never know what to expect. If only this
war would end, and I could come back to you. Someone had
a radio on the other day and it was playing our song, "Love
Is Blue." I got all choked up and had to walk away. You
mean so much to me, Kitten. As soon as I get back, let's
plan our future together. I want to spend the rest of my life
with you.
Love, Joel

But instead of swooning over his words, I felt confused.

"Love Is Blue" had been my song *before* I met Joel. The music moved me so much that I would dance around the room almost in a trance, brimming with joy, intoxicated with my freedom of movement. In those moments I needed nothing. I felt complete. When I had tried to share with Joel how I felt, the words had always eluded me. But now that he was gone, I felt a gaping hole inside of me that even my favorite song couldn't fill. I didn't like feeling this dependent on anyone, but at the same time, I didn't know how to stop it. I couldn't deny that I was afraid of losing myself—and my newfound freedom—to the dream of marrying Joel.

Traveling seemed to help, so I moved around a lot, exploring new places after leaving New York. Joel was always with me in my heart, but I was also on a mission. I believed I could cram every new experience into my life while Joel was away, and that when he came back, I'd be ready to settle down and marry him.

Dear Joel,
Guess what! I was talking to a girl in New York and she
told me about an agency that helps people get temporary
secretarial jobs in London. They will help me get a visa

*and find a place to live and everything. This is going to be
an exciting adventure! I want to explore the world before
we're together again. I don't want to miss anything. I can't
wait to tell you all about it. I miss you.*
Love, Jan

The truth was, I was terrified that my two very different
dreams of marrying Joel and being free to explore the world
would tear me apart. I was drawn toward Joel and thought I
wanted the traditional marriage with the white picket fence.
But now that I was faced with the opportunity, I realized that
I also needed to be free to explore. I wanted to find my place
in the universe, and my parents' marriage was never far from
my mind, reminding me that I didn't want that kind of life.

Dear Kitten,
*You seem so far away. I'm counting the days until I hold
you in my arms again. Please send me a picture to keep
under my pillow. I love you so much.*
Love, Joel

I sent him an airbrushed portrait of me with my hair
looking perfect. I didn't realize what he really wanted was a
risqué photo of me, like the ones some soldiers lusted over.

Dear Joel,
*I have an opportunity to travel through Europe for a few
months. I'll be leaving this summer. I hope I'll be back in the
States by the time you get back. I hate being so far away
from you. I'm going to take a boat to Paris, and then travel
down to Rome.*
I love you.
Jan

Traveling in Europe, I got caught up in the flood of hippies wandering around looking for themselves. I felt I belonged with them and didn't want to leave. I also began to feel time closing in on me.

Dear Jan,
I'll be home in a couple of weeks. Where will you be? I
want to see you as soon as I get back. I have so many plans
for us. Disneyland, camping, movies, hamburgers, french
fries, and running naked in the woods. I can't wait.
Love, Joel

Joel returned from Vietnam.
But I stayed in Europe a bit longer.
I couldn't help but think, *I might never be this free again.*

5

MARRIAGE OR MIRAGE?

*W*HEN JOEL RETURNED FROM VIETNAM IN 1969, I didn't see him for a month. He was stationed in Fort Huachuca, Arizona, hundreds of miles away from my home in Los Angeles. But as soon as he knew I was back, he found a way to come and visit me.

"You're putting me on, right?" Joel said, his expression one of disbelief when I told him I hadn't slept with anyone in my travels. "Not in New York, and not in Europe? My God, Jan, all that time on the road, all those men. I'm sure they wanted to get in your pants. And you're still a virgin?"

Yes, I'm still a virgin. The curse of being a good Catholic girl.

I had certainly been tempted. But I remained faithful to Joel.

Maybe I should have had more fun, I thought. Instead I said, "I was saving myself for you."

His look of disappointment surprised me, until it hit me: he wanted me to have experience, like him. He didn't want a naïve girl; he wanted a worldly woman. I suddenly wondered why I had saved myself for him.

I guess I thought it would mean something to him. I learned in church that marriage is a sacred commitment and that a girl should save herself for her husband, as a precious gift to be opened only by him.

But the truth was that in my travels, I had come face to face with the phenomenon of the times: free love. People were now exploring their sexuality without the need for commitment. At the time, I was both attracted to and repulsed by this. I blamed my Catholic upbringing for the latter and began to fantasize about what it would be like to be in an open relationship.

If I'm free, I reasoned, *I won't be trapped, like Mom.*

SOON AFTER I DROPPED THE BOMB ON JOEL THAT I HAD saved myself for him, I talked to my friend Jeannie about my dilemma and my virgin status. Jeannie had been dating a guy for over a year, and was, of course, sleeping with him. She said, "Jan, what are you waiting for?"

I still believed that marriage was the most sacred union two people could experience, going through life together as equal partners. But I was admittedly unclear about the balance of each partner's responsibilities. The chaos of living with an angry husband and out-of-control kids who were expected to be perfect wouldn't work for me. I wanted my own life. But I also wanted to be taken care of.

"I don't know," I shrugged. "I thought I was supposed to get married first. I thought I was supposed to wait for my wedding night."

"Did he save himself for you?"

"Oh," I stuttered, "I don't know … I guess not."

"Of course he didn't," Jeannie confirmed with a huff. "He's a guy, and he's in the Army. How can you know for sure if he's the right person for you if you don't sleep with him?"

Soon after that, I reasoned that I had waited long enough. I went to the doctor, got birth control pills, and told Joel I was ready but that I needed time to make sure the pills kicked in. I was determined not to get pregnant, which I believed would ruin my life for sure. The pills made me nauseated, but it was a side effect I was willing to put up with.

I flew to Fort Huachuca where Joel was stationed, and after picking me up at the airport, he drove straight to the river and laid out a blanket.

"Joel, it's cold," I objected. *My first time is NOT going to be like this.*

I wasn't comfortable being out in the open, but instead of being understanding, Joel picked up the blanket and threw it in the car. As he drove to a nearby motel, I could tell he was angry.

Upon arrival, the desk clerk asked how old I was. I knew I looked young, which only added to the embarrassment and shame I was already feeling. *Damn the church.* I felt so unclear in that moment about what was expected of me; my mind was telling me one thing, while my skin was tingling with desire like an open wound needing to be soothed.

Here we were, in a sleazy motel in Arizona, about to have sex. Joel was trying to be gentle but my body was saying no. Too many years of being the good girl, of saving myself, created mixed feelings that swirled in my head. When Joel finally gave up, I felt secretly relieved that I was unable to complete the act. Staring at the ceiling, I figured I was probably one of the last twenty-two-year-old virgins around.

After a short time, Joel thought we should try again. After the third attempt, there was finally penetration. It hurt, but I was grateful for the breakthrough. I hoped it would get better, easier, and more enjoyable, but that night, I was left wondering if that was all there was to sex.

Despite the rocky start to our first time together, Joel softened as we lay in each other's arms.

"So what should we do when I get out of the Army?" he asked.

"I've always wanted to travel across the United States," I said with enthusiasm.

"Let's do it, Kitten. I would love to do that with you. We can visit my relatives in different parts of the country." He sat up on one elbow. "When I get out, let's get jobs for a while, save our money, and then sell everything and travel for three months. We can buy a van and sleep in it the nights we're not staying with relatives."

"Yes!" I said, happy he seemed to be reading my mind.

"The thing is," Joel continued, "it would be a lot cheaper for us to get married now while I'm still in the Army. Then they would pay more of our expenses."

With the excitement of adventure ahead, I couldn't see any reason not to get married. Joel and I would be together, like I knew we would be anyway, only we'd have more money and I would get to travel. It sounded perfect, but still wanting my freedom, I couldn't help but wonder if it would really be enough.

Maybe it's time to be bold.

"Joel," I said, "I want to be with you … and if getting married will save us money, then okay, let's get married. But I need to let you know how I feel about marriage. I need my independence. I need to know that I can be myself and do whatever I want to do. I want to experience more of life, and I don't know where it will take me. So if we get married, I'd like us to have an open marriage."

I paused for effect, but Joel said nothing, so I continued.

"If either of us finds that we want to go somewhere else or be with someone else, we should be able to do that. I don't want jealousy or possession to be a part of our marriage. Let's just do what we want and be honest about it."

"Okay, Kitten," he readily agreed. "I love you. Will you marry me?"

He was smiling and had responded so quickly and easily that I wondered if he understood what I said. Then I thought, *Of course he's smiling. I just offered him a man's dream deal.* Ultimately, though, it didn't matter. I knew what I wanted and those were my terms.

"Yes, I will," I said, feeling remarkably loved and free all at once.

I WAS EXCITED ABOUT SHARING MY NEWS WITH THE people I was closest to, expecting them to be happy for me. But when I told Christine that Joel and I were engaged, all she said was, "Oh?"

"What's wrong?" I said. "Aren't you happy for me? I'm getting married!"

"Of course," Christine said hesitantly. "If it makes you happy then I'm happy for you. But just so you know, he did flirt with me the first time I met him. You know what that means, don't you?"

"Oh, come on," I said defensively. "Joel is a flirt, but he's mine, and he loves me, so I'm not worried about it. Besides, I don't believe in being possessive."

That's when she gave me that look that says, "I have way more to say, but I know you aren't going to listen, so I'll just stifle myself."

I could feel my heart beating faster to the point of wanting to lash out at her, but I didn't. I knew she might be right, but I was not about to give her concerns any credence and destroy my illusion of "love conquering all" in my fragile world.

Unlike Christine, my family was happy for me, especially my sisters. They enjoyed Joel's flirtatious ways, which didn't bother me because I knew he was only interested in me. Of course he would probably still flirt with other women after we got married, but I was used to that. I trusted him. And we'd tell each other everything. We were both on board with having an open marriage.

THE WEDDING WAS SIMPLE, SURROUNDED BY OUR FAMILIES and some friends in a small, open chapel encircled by lush greenery. I had found a sense of peace in reading Khalil Gibran's *The Prophet*, so I asked for readings from his poetry—Gibran's words gave me comfort in the difficult process of commitment I was about to step into.

> *Let there be spaces in your togetherness and let the winds of the heavens dance between you. Love one another but make not a bond of love: let it rather be a moving sea between the shores of your souls.*

I knew deep inside that this kind of love was possible; I also knew it was the only kind of love I was willing to commit to in matrimony. I had informed the minister of the conditions of our marriage, and he had accused me of advocating free love, which at the time was rampant. Yes, I was advocating free love, but I didn't see anything wrong with that.

I had no idea what I was getting myself into.

JOEL AND I HONEYMOONED FOR A FEW DAYS IN THE mountains of Southern California and then packed all our wedding gifts and belongings into a trailer. Hitching it to the car, we drove off to Fort Huachuca, where Joel had found us a place to live in the mountains, away from the base.

Driving into town, my eyes grew wide as I noted only one gas station, one movie theatre, and few people milling about, a far cry from the glitz and glamour of Los Angeles where everything was available.

My mind began to race. *What have I done? How can I stay here? Why did we bring all our stuff? Why didn't he tell me it was like this? How will I find my freedom here?*

When Joel drove up to a dingy, dirty, one-room concrete cabin, I immediately thought, *this can't be right.* I wanted to turn around and go home. As I wondered why I had gotten married, I told Joel I couldn't stay unless he found us a decent place to live.

Joel comforted me and said he was sorry, that he wasn't thinking straight, that he loved me and wanted me to be happy. That helped.

We spent the next few days scrubbing down the entire cabin just to make it livable. Dad had always made us thoroughly clean places we moved in and out of throughout my childhood, and I felt better when everything was clean. Besides, Joel promised to find us a better place, so this was only temporary. We kept our wedding gifts tucked away in boxes in a corner of the room until true to his word, Joel found us a bigger cabin close to the mountains, where we stayed until the end of Joel's commitment to the military.

Around the Army base, I quickly learned that Joel was well known when one of the wives seemed a bit taken aback at the sight of me.

"Wow, Joel," she said, "I'm not used to seeing you with someone. You're usually by yourself."

Her husband chuckled under his breath, although I thought it actually sounded more like a snicker.

Joel had told me about sometimes going to a border town in Mexico, and I figured he simply needed to let go and have fun—which probably involved women, getting drunk, and maybe even drugs.

But he's with me now, I reminded myself. I was too naïve to even consider what might have really been going on down there.

Boring as it was in the small town near the base, there was a lot going on to keep us distracted. Drugs were rampant and I was soon exposed to marijuana and LSD, which were a normal part of the Army culture at that time. Drugs had been plentiful in Europe too, especially marijuana. I tried it a few times, but it only led to coughing.

Once I got beyond the coughing, though, I regularly smoked grass with Joel and his friends. I discovered a relaxation and humorous attitude toward life that I had never experienced. I also learned that Joel had done LSD many times and that the people living next door had a generous supply. Despite telling Joel I didn't think it was a good idea, I was curious.

One day I asked Joel if he would consider giving me half a tab of LSD with the condition that he not take any and that he be there with me. He agreed and stayed with me through the entire trip, the chords of Pink Floyd setting the tone, as I watched Joel turn into a skeleton, the walls breathing in and out as if they were alive. Then I felt like I was pregnant and getting bigger and bigger. Hours later, when I finally came down, I was glad to be back in the reality I was used to.

Joel shared with me flashbacks from previous acid trips, like the time he walked toward his car and tried to put the key in but saw nothing but a pile of nuts and bolts, or how he and his friends would play chicken with cars coming from the opposite direction. After hearing his stories and having my own bizarre experience, I pleaded with him to not do LSD anymore and he agreed.

We were both counting the days when we would be able to leave the desolate place that had become our home and travel the country. Freedom was all I wanted, so along with the security of being married, I couldn't wait for our adventure. Joel seemed to share my excitement in our common goal.

LESS THAN A YEAR AFTER WE WERE MARRIED, JOEL WAS out of the Army and we moved back home. We found a small apartment in Santa Ana, near Joel's family, who provided plenty of free meals so we could save for our trip. We both got jobs we didn't like and were relieved when, after about a year, we had saved enough money to quit. We sold or gave away almost all our belongings and hit the road in a brand-new green 1972 Dodge van with leather seats and a designer stripe around it, taking little with us but some clothes, our floppy leather hats, and enough money to keep us going for a few months. We were hippies on the run.

I loved being on the road. We spent the first part of the trip exploring national parks, then we headed to the Midwest, where most of Joel's relatives lived. Though usually pretty manic about my appearance, I eventually stopped being so concerned about how I looked and what I was wearing. That added to the sense of freedom I craved, and though it was an adjustment, I loved it.

Joel was a good travel companion who took care of me and made me feel safe. And his family was wonderful too. Every time we arrived at one of their homes, they welcomed us with open arms and good food, including fresh produce from the garden, which I had never tasted before. Being raised in Hollywood, I thought everything came from the grocery store. The fresh vegetables were a far cry from the canned peas Mom used to serve.

I began to sincerely enjoy country life, which was relaxed and more laid-back than living in the city. Though I still longed for the excitement of L.A., I enjoyed doing nothing much but eating, taking walks, playing games, and spending time with Joel and his family. The nights we didn't stay with his relatives, we set ourselves up in campgrounds and slept in the back of our van.

Life was simple for a while.

Over time, I learned that Joel had an edge, one that reminded me of my father. But unlike Dad, Joel brushed things off with sarcastic humor. Far from lightening the mood, however, his behavior made me uneasy and caused my body to tense up.

In addition to his acerbity, he wanted sex—every night. While he turned me on with his charming smile and loving caresses, and I sincerely loved being with him, sex every night felt like an obligation. I didn't want to be like Mom, but appeasing him kept the peace, so I conceded. Afterwards, we were like best friends, cuddling and talking about everything. He was more understanding in those days, doing his best to please me, as long as he was taken care of first.

When we finally reached the east coast and called on some of my relatives on Dad's side of the family, the feel of our "down-home life on the road" changed dramatically. These people were rich and not as warm and welcoming as Joel's family; in fact, I shouldn't have been surprised when most of them were unavailable and on trips to St. Croix or occupied with their privately schooled children. I had stayed with some of them when I first went to New York, so I knew what they were like, but after rooming for a little while with my cousin and his young family, we felt a bit out of place and decided to head back west.

Three months after leaving, we landed once again in the Los Angeles area. Not having planned much beyond this, we had nowhere to live, no jobs to return to.

We found ourselves lost together.

UNTIL WE GOT OUR BEARINGS AND FOUND WORK AND A place to live, we moved in with Joel's parents. Both Joel and I were holding out for the perfect jobs—like many twenty-somethings, we wanted exciting careers that paid a lot of money. But after months of searching and no place of our own yet, we realized that we were going to have to take work where we could find it. Joel got his old job back at the telephone company, and I landed a secretarial position at a chemical laboratory. Soon after, we found an apartment in Orange County near Joel's family.

That's when the real test of our open marriage began.

As we started to mingle with new people, we accepted invitations to parties from friends at our respective jobs and those who lived in our apartment complex. The air was abuzz with the fresh, exciting contacts we were making as our social circle began expanding.

One night, at one of those parties, Joel took his usual position in the middle of a group of women while I stood across the room talking to Bob, a mutual friend.

"Have you noticed what your husband is doing?" Bob asked, his voice ringing with concern.

"No. Well, I did see him talking to some woman, if that's what you mean."

"Aren't you concerned? Jealous?"

"No, not really. He's just talking and having a good time."

"Jan," he said, leaning toward me, "she unbuttoned his shirt and they just went into one of the bedrooms."

"So what?" I said with a nonchalant air. "He's free to do whatever he wants while we're here. He's going home with me."

"But what about him being with another woman? Doesn't it bother you?"

"I'm okay," I said.

But Bob didn't buy it. He was relentless with his questions, making me aware that I was less comfortable than I realized with Joel's behavior. Insecurities I thought I had under control welled to the surface, and I knew I had to find a distraction. *Two could play at this game.* Bob was a good-looking guy, so I focused on him. The more concern he expressed, the more attracted I became.

I found myself wishing he would just grab me and take me somewhere to make mad, passionate love to me. But Bob did not respond the way I wanted him to. He seemed to have more respect for my marriage than either Joel or I did.

At that point, I left Bob for a while and began flirting with a married man whose wife was out of town. *If Joel can be free, then so can I. Isn't that what we agreed to? That we could both do our own thing?*

"Are you here alone?" he asked me.

"No. I came with my husband, but I'm not with him right now." I raised my eyebrows in a confident invitation.

He handed me his card. "I'd like it if you'd call me at work some time."

I wasn't really attracted to him, but I loved the attention. Giggling, I stuck the card in my bra and walked away.

That night, as Joel and I drove home, I questioned him about his disappearance with the other woman. He'd had too many beers, as usual, and was defensive.

"It was nothing, Jan. We were just talking."

I was afraid to push, but I also wanted to get to the truth. Fortunately, the alcohol I'd drunk gave me permission to do that. After all, we promised each other honesty, and if this open relationship was going to work, Joel owed me at least that much.

"Then why did you go into the bedroom with her?"

"Jeez, Jan. We were just playing around. What's with all the questions all of a sudden? And what were you doing with Bob?"

My face flushed as I thought about Bob and how much I thought I desired him. I decided not to respond as I questioned our open marriage, the kind that got people into trouble, the kind that could so easily perpetrate the jealousy I had begun to feel.

By the time we got home, the tension between us was as taut as a violin string. We lay on opposite sides of the bed, each of us in our own worlds, separated by the fear of how our true feelings might upset the balance of our marriage. Neither of us had any idea how to do this. *Maybe all the people who questioned why we were married had a point.*

6

BACKFIRE

I FOUND MYSELF PAYING MORE ATTENTION TO JOEL'S whereabouts—he was working the late shift in a machine shop, and sometimes he wouldn't come home until morning. The first time this happened, our conversation went like this:

"Where have you been?"

"I was at the beach."

"The beach. Why?"

"I needed to think."

I didn't believe him, but I let it go.

A few nights later, we went through the same scenario.

"So where were you this time?" I asked, trying to appear indifferent. But I could see from his face that he'd caught the irritation in my voice.

"I had to work overtime."

I gave him a look and dropped the subject. Then later, when he climbed into bed, I turned away and pretended to be asleep. The distance between us was growing wider each day.

One morning, as he rolled in with liquor still on his breath, I asked him point blank, "Are you seeing someone else?"

"No, Jan, I'm not. Why would you think that? I told you. I've been working hard and sometimes I go to the beach to unwind."

I told myself I was crazy, that he must be telling the truth. I didn't want to believe he was lying to me. But something felt off.

Another morning he came in even later than usual. This time, I had been waiting to hear his key in the door. I didn't want to rock the boat, but I couldn't help myself. I sat up in bed.

"Joel, please just tell me the truth. Are you seeing someone?"

Without hesitation, he said, "Yes, I am."

My mouth dropped open and my stomach tightened up so intensely that I crouched over in pain. Even though I suspected as much and my body sensed something was wrong for a while, the truth gutted me.

I sat up slowly, fighting back tears. "Who is she?"

"Someone I work with."

He seemed so flippant about it. "So why did you lie to me?"

"I didn't lie to you."

"No? You told me you had to work late and that you were going to the beach after that."

"That's true."

"What do you mean, 'that's true'? You just admitted there's someone else!"

"Well," he said sheepishly, "She lives in Huntington Beach."

He sounded like a little boy, afraid to tell his mommy the whole truth about what he had done.

"Can I meet her?"

"You want to meet her?"

"Yes."

"I don't know if that would be the best thing," he said, shoving his hands into his pockets.

"Why not?"

He looked away.

"Why do you want to be with her?" I persisted.

"Well," he said, "she does some things you won't do."

I didn't need to ask what those things were. I was well aware of my sexual inhibitions. Joel had pressured me for years about doing things I wasn't comfortable doing. In a way, I actually felt relieved that the pressure was off.

"I'm going to go sleep on the couch tonight," Joel said.

"Okay. Go ahead."

Alone in bed, I sobbed uncontrollably until I finally felt nothing left inside and drifted off to sleep. Despite having agreed to an open marriage, I felt like everything that was supposed to be my future was falling apart.

The next day, I tried to be cool about the whole thing. But I wasn't going to take no for an answer about meeting the woman who was having an affair with my husband. I told myself that the main reason I didn't like what was going on was that Joel had lied to me. He still didn't like the idea, but he relunctantly agreed.

Soon after, he brought her home one evening, unannounced. As he walked in with a guilty look on his face, she hung back a bit, seemingly unsure about my reaction.

"Jan," he said, "this is Laurie."

She was beautiful and sexy and rather exotic, with deep brown eyes and long, curly brown hair. Even though I felt I should automatically hate her, I was intrigued by her and wanted to know her better. Who was this woman who was sleeping with my husband, giving him what he wanted, things I was unwilling to do?

"Laurie's had some bad luck," Joel said awkwardly. "Her car broke down and she's been evicted from her apartment. I'm going to help her find a place to stay."

"She can stay with us for a while," I volunteered. The words shocked even me as they fell out of my mouth.

"Are you serious?" Joel's eyes widened as he looked back and forth, trying to read both our reactions simultaneously.

"Yes," I said, feeling very mature about it all.

"That's very nice of you," Laurie said.

"But I have one requirement," I said. "You guys can't sleep with each other. We can all be friends, but Laurie, you'll sleep on the couch."

Joel stood there dumbfounded as Laurie nodded in agreement.

The next night, we went to dinner at a private club where Laurie got us in because she knew the waiter. Afterward, we came back home and stayed up talking and laughing for hours. We were getting along well, and I had to admit I liked her. Laurie was definitely adding some excitement to our boring lives. She was so free and open with her body that Joel wasn't the only one affected by the steamy sensuality that oozed so easily and naturally from her.

Not too long after Laurie moved in, I went to bed early one night. When I came out an hour later to get a drink of water, I found her and Joel on the floor in each other's arms. They didn't see me, so I snuck back into the bedroom. I lay still for hours, unable to sleep, listening to them talking and giggling. I couldn't hear them clearly over the slow, romantic, sensual music they were playing that works so well for making love. I was curious, but I was too scared to venture into my own living room.

When Joel cuddled up beside me in the early morning, my body tightened up and my eyes popped open. I stayed still until I couldn't stand being in bed any longer and got up. In the living room I found Laurie sleeping on the couch, a contented smile on her face. I felt betrayed.

THE NEXT DAY I HAD LUNCH WITH JEANNIE, WHO WAS appalled at the living arrangements I'd encouraged.

"Jan," she said, "what are you doing? How can you stand having the woman your husband is having an affair with in your home? If that happened to me, I'd bolt and take him for everything he has."

"No, it's fine," I defended. "I'm having a good time. We all get along well, and besides, he's not sleeping with her." I knew better but didn't want to admit it.

Jeannie tilted her head and squinted. "Jan, wake up. He's a man. Of course he's sleeping with her—every chance he gets. She's a slut, don't you see that? She just wants your man." She put her glass down. "And by the way, Joel has flirted with me. Many times."

I looked away. Jeannie had told me this before, and I remembered other friends—like Christine—who had warned me that Joel was flirting with them. I pondered all the women I knew Joel had been friendly with and wondered how many more there were. Then I thought, *How many of them has he slept with?*

Joel tried to justify his relationship with Laurie by encouraging me to go out with other men. Although in some ways I found the idea intriguing, I was not yet ready. At the same time, though, it was becoming clear that Laurie wanted Joel for herself. We were a month into our arrangement and I had grown tired of playing. I knew I couldn't trust Joel with Laurie and was afraid to leave them alone.

One evening I caught her giving him that "let's do it now" look at the dinner table. When he averted his eyes in obvious discomfort, I had to laugh. The threesome was backfiring on him too. Now he had two women watching his every move.

Undressing to go to bed alone one night, I wondered whether this situation was just a convenient way to escape the tension that had built between Joel and me over our married life. As I drifted off, I allowed myself to travel to that peaceful place where angels surrounded me with their sweet song, the way Mom used to sing me to sleep in her comforting voice. "Jan is my darling, my darling, my darling. Jan is my darling, my darling little girl."

Then I heard, *"Jan, you deserve to be treated with love and respect."*

But I wasn't in a place where I could believe it.

I had to face the fact that this open marriage arrangement wasn't working out the way I had planned. In fact, it was blowing up in my face. In spite of being confused about my marriage, however, I knew one thing for sure: I did not want that woman to have my man. I eventually told Laurie it was time for her to leave, and Joel agreed. But I knew this wouldn't fix things between Joel and me. I wasn't sure anything would.

7

STEPPING OUT

SOME TIME AFTER LAURIE MOVED OUT, JOEL AND I were invited to a cocktail party. Joel couldn't go because of his job, so I decided to go by myself. The party, which was being sponsored by a well-known real estate company, was being held in an office building in well-to-do Newport Beach. If nothing else, maybe I would meet some interesting people.

When I arrived, I didn't see any familiar faces, but I reminded myself that I was there to expand my social life and resisted my usual urge to ditch a situation like this and simply leave. Scanning the venue for a friendly face, I noticed a crowd gathered around a man in the middle of the room. Intrigued by the sound of his voice, I headed that way to see what was happening.

"Your mind is powerful, and you can program it to achieve anything you want," I heard him say as I approached.

His words struck me. Other ventures of Joel's and mine hadn't gone well for us, but there had to be something to this idea of unlimited possibilities. I joined the crowd to hear more.

The man lit a cigarette and then proceeded to stub it out in the palm of his hand, making no sound or facial expression of pain.

"Wow! How did he do that?" I remarked out loud.

As he stood there, remaining quiet as people whispered amongst themselves, I couldn't take my eyes off him. Overweight, with a large face and a big nose, he was hardly attractive. Drops of sweat rolled down his temples, and every now and then he would wipe his brow with a handkerchief. Yet, a magnetic quality about him drew me in.

The cigarette trick had been good bait, and a larger crowd had grown around him. We were entering the world of magic, where anything was possible—a far cry from the limitations of my small life. I didn't know it then, but like Alice in Wonderland, I was poised at the entrance of the rabbit hole.

For his next trick he asked for a volunteer and chose a young girl.

"So what's your name?" he asked.

"Jenny."

"Jenny. Pretty name for a pretty girl. And you seem very brave too," he said. "Now, Jenny, I don't think we've ever met. Do you recall meeting me anywhere before?"

"No," she laughed. "What's your name?"

"Rocko," he replied. "So, Jenny, what I want you to do is hold your arm out in front of you and try to keep me from pushing it down."

Jenny held her arm out straight as Rocko had asked. He gently pressed on her arm with one hand and her arm fell with ease.

Tilting his head down at her, he rolled his eyes. "Now tell the truth," he said. "Did you feel me using my strength to push your arm down?"

"No," she admitted. "You didn't push hard at all."

"Right," he said, swiping his brow. "I exerted almost no pressure at all. You just wimped out."

The crowd roared, and the girl blushed.

"But you're stronger than me," she said, giggling.

"That's okay," he said. "Big men wimp out the same way. Don't worry about it. Now, Jenny, you're going to get a chance to show us what you're made of."

His voice flowed smooth as buttermilk as he focused his penetrating blue eyes directly on her.

"This is your opportunity to shine. I want you to think of something you really want, and imagine that it's right there at the end of your arm. And you have to keep your arm straight in order to get it."

My body tingled with curiosity to know more about this man. I watched as Jenny focused on the end of her arm and Rocko pushed down. Amazing. This time she was able to hold her arm steady.

What kind of a trick was this?

I want to try it.

I stepped forward and asked him if he would do it with me. He agreed and waved me toward him. The first time I held my arm up, he pressed only lightly on it and it dropped. Then he told me to focus on the end of my arm, breathe deeply, and think of something I really wanted.

It worked. My arm didn't budge.

"That's how powerful your mind is," he said. "If you focus it on what you want and make the decision not to back down or let anything get in your way, you can achieve it. You are unstoppable."

A shiver ran through me as I felt my awareness opening to the notion that endless possibilities awaited me.

Despite his slovenly appearance, I was powerfully attracted to this man, and I hung around longer than I normally would have. After his demonstration, he invited me to a talk he was giving the following night. I knew that nothing could keep me away.

When I got home, I tried to share with Joel what I had experienced, but all I could focus on was the incredible excitement I felt at the thought of seeing Rocko again. When I mentioned going to his talk the next evening, Joel reminded me that we were supposed to go to his sister's birthday party.

My face and shoulders deflated. "Do you mind if I don't go to the party?" I asked.

Searching for a reaction of some kind from my husband, I wondered if he could see through me, to the giddiness I was trying—unsuccessfully, I thought—to hide for another man. But Joel merely shrugged and said his sister's party wasn't a big deal, seeming not to care that I wouldn't be there.

The next night, after Joel left for the party, I got dressed to go to the meeting. Standing in front of the mirror, all I felt was frustration—I was too short, I couldn't find the right clothes to wear, and my hair stuck out in all the wrong places.

When I finally found an outfit I liked, I saw that my eyes were sparkling and my skin was glowing. I felt like I was in love again. My irresistible draw to Rocko made my body feel like it was on fire; my mouth was watering and my knees were weak. I couldn't get over how he was affecting me even when I wasn't in his presence. Then I realized it was because I desired what he represented to me: confidence, freedom, and the possibility of having all I ever wanted.

8

*

LOST

*T*HE INTRODUCTORY MEETING FOR ROCKO'S MIND control class took place in a small office complex. As I walked into the room, I felt a surge of energy shoot through my body and sat down next to an attractive woman who appeared as excited as I was. A few more people came in, but the group remained small.

Aren't a lot of people eager to learn about this? I wondered, having expected a throng to be present.

After Rocko walked in, he introduced himself and did the same tricks as at the cocktail party, making me wonder if he had anything else to offer and if it was worth my time. Then he delivered the punch.

"Do you realize how powerful your imagination is?" he said. "You can turn your life around—all you have to do is allow your imagination to create what you want. Once you learn to control your mind, you can change your perspective on anything." His voice then took on a more intimate tone. "I'm going to tell you a story that will show you what I mean."

Everyone grew quiet.

"There was a community that had been devastated by fire. Reporters were having a field day talking to the people who had just lost their homes. You know how they like to empha-size the tragedy of it all."

My gaze was drawn to Rocko's deep blue eyes. I felt as though he were speaking directly to me, as if I was the only person in the room.

He continued, "One reporter walked up to a man who was sitting near the ruins of his house with his family. 'Excuse me, sir,' he said. 'Is this the worst day of your life?' He was hoping for the usual tears and sad story, but that's not what he got. Instead, the man stood up proudly and said, 'Quite the con-trary. This is the best day of my life. This fire has opened up a new world for me. Today I can start over. I can create a new life for my family and myself. And I'm more grateful than ever before for my family and friends, and all the things that are really important to me.' The reporter then quietly backed away, not knowing how to respond. He was so programmed to look for bad news that this man's story caught him off guard."

He glanced around the small audience.

"So, ladies and gentlemen, that is how powerful our minds can be. We can turn any situation in our lives, no matter how bad others might think it might be, into an opportunity to create more happiness and abundance."

Wow! I thought, *I've never thought of things that way before.*

Rocko went on to announce that he was offering a six-week course to teach us how to reprogram our minds and use our imaginations to live a more balanced and positive life.

"Six weeks. Wow! That's all?" I blurted out.

"Yes," he said.

I was in. "Where do I sign?"

I HUNG AROUND AFTER THE MEETING, HOPING TO SPEND some time with Rocko. The woman sitting next to me lingered as well. My body was shivering uncontrollably, a sure sign that I was in deep and unable to turn back. I was afraid my face would turn beet-red, as it always did when a man I was attracted to paid attention to me. At last Rocko came over and the three of us talked for a while.

Finally, the other woman left, and Rocko asked to walk me out to my car.

"Yes, thank you," I said, feeling the heat rising to my face. I hoped he wouldn't notice.

When he invited me out for a drink, I accepted without hesitation, and we went to a small neighborhood bar down the street. For reasons I didn't completely understand, I couldn't get close enough to this man. Even still, I didn't hide that I was married, mentioning that my husband was at his sister's birthday party. He only tipped his head back with an "Oh," giving me no indication if that mattered or not. Consumed with the spirited attention I was receiving from this man, I pushed away an annoying tinge of guilt and was completely unconcerned about getting home.

"Jan," he said, "do you realize how beautiful you are, and how intelligent?"

I felt like he must have been talking to another woman named Jan and was tempted to turn around to see her for myself.

"I can't wait to see where you are six weeks from now, after you take my class," he continued.

I couldn't believe it was only going to take six weeks to change my whole outlook on life and make me believe I was beautiful and intelligent. Yet, coming from Rocko, the words sank in. He seemed to have some magical power over me. Then, he put his arms around me and leaned in to kiss me. When he pulled away, he looked into my eyes and said, "Jan, do you have any idea who you are?"

"What do you mean?" I asked, dazed.

Instead of answering me with words, he began to touch me in places and in ways I had never been touched before, with just the right amount of pressure to send sparks shooting through my body. In a secluded corner of that dark neighborhood bar, I surrendered, melting into him.

Oh my goodness. And we still have our clothes on.

This was like a romance novel. I looked into his eyes for a moment, lost. Then I thought of Joel. I loved my husband, but I wasn't feeling that exciting tingly sensation with him anymore. Rocko's touch sent me beyond anything I had ever experienced before.

"I should go home," I said at last, lost in Rocko's spell. I knew in that moment that I would do anything for this man. But I also felt a stab of shame.

By the time I got home, it was after midnight. I opened the door as quietly as possible and tiptoed into the bedroom. Joel was already in bed, but awake.

"Hi Kitten," he said. "Where've you been?"

I told him I had gone out for a drink with Rocko.

"How was it? Were there other people there with you?"

"No, we were alone," I said casually, but I knew my face betrayed my guilt.

Joel didn't seem to notice. He turned over and I climbed into bed beside him. I wanted to tell him everything, to see how he would react. Actually, I wanted him to be jealous, but he went right to sleep.

As I lay there beside my husband, remembering the sensations I had felt with Rocko, I wondered if I should feel guilty for what I'd done. *I'm married. I'm only supposed to be with my husband. But he's played around with other women. And how can anything that feels that good be wrong? Plus, we do have an open marriage, right?*

The morals of my Catholic upbringing loomed large in

my mind. Even though the church's rules no longer made sense, I couldn't seem to shake them.

EACH NEW WEEK WITH ROCKO IN THE MIND CONTROL class was more exciting than the last.

I quickly discovered that my childhood conditioning had left me with some highly limiting beliefs. Not only did I not believe I deserved wealth and love, but I didn't think I was smart enough to achieve or receive either one. I had grown up thinking only rich people got what they wanted out of life, and I had resigned myself to living the way I was brought up—"Too much month at the end of the money," as Dad often said.

As my mind opened to new possibilities, I became even more obsessed with Rocko. Truthfully, I just wanted him to take over my mind and make the change for me, to transfer whatever he had into me without my having to do the work. Of course that wasn't possible, but the six weeks of exercises felt like too much for me. I was the impatient type who wanted instant gratification and growth.

"Take a deep breath," he instructed. "Now, as I count to five, you will descend deeper and deeper into your mind.

"One, imagine you are walking through a tunnel that gets darker the farther in you go.

"Two, with each step you take you are going deeper, and feeling more relaxed.

"Three, you are now feeling more relaxed then you've ever felt in your entire life.

"Four, you are going even deeper.

"Five, every breath you take brings you deeper and deeper. Your body is completely relaxed, and your mind is open."

Lost in the magic of his voice, I was a goner.

"Now imagine yourself walking out of the tunnel into a beautiful, lush garden that belongs to you."

I pictured myself walking across a cute little bridge into an area by a stream, surrounded by lovely green trees and brightly colored flowers of every kind. I sat down in a small alcove, just the right size for me, supported and caressed by the rocks and protected by the trees that encircled me. The temperature was perfect. The steady flow of the stream put me in a playful and creative mood.

Then I heard his soothing voice gently guiding me back to the room.

Rocko said that any time we wanted to relax, all we had to do was say the word "garden" to ourselves and it would take us back to the experience of being in our own special garden. He was right. It worked for me then, and it still works for me today.

From then on, I followed Rocko around, well beyond the six-week course, agreeing to work for him and his amazing self-help business. I wanted everyone to know about it and be a part of it. As a result, I became his top salesperson in a short amount of time.

In spite of being wrapped up in my loyalty and enthusiasm, however, I quickly learned that there was more to his business dealings than helping people.

Rocko would entice people to invest in his company, which he promised would make millions. That Christmas, he convinced a man he had been hounding for a while to invest. I stood there as he wrote out a check and handed it to Rocko. As soon as the man left, Rocko turned to me and said, "All right, let's go Christmas shopping."

I tried to convince myself that this was a legitimate business, but the truth was, his immorality excited me. I had been such a good girl all my life and I was tired of it. Being good seemed to have brought me nothing. It was time to break all the rules, or at least be around someone who did. I was making money and Joel didn't question me, so I overlooked Rocko's shady dealings and prided myself in being his "right-hand woman."

On top of his illegitimate business practices, I discovered that Rocko was married with a daughter and that he had a girlfriend on the side. When I met his wife and daughter, I got the impression that his wife was irritated by the other women, but that she tolerated his behavior to keep her family more or less together.

Rocko's girlfriend Gina had lost her husband the previous year and inherited a sum of money that left her financially independent. He clearly used her for her money, telling me, "You can fall in love with anyone, so why not choose someone with money?"

It reminded me of my grandmother, who used to say, "It's just as easy to fall in love with a rich man as a poor man." In other words, "Don't waste your time. Go for the rich one."

At some point, Rocko invited a group of us to a retreat in Catalina where he was claiming to be psychic. Joel came along, kind of reluctantly; he was also a bit taken by Rocko, but I was the one who had grown more and more dependent on his validation and guidance. I wanted him to fix my life for me, and I was constantly pushing him for answers or predictions about my future.

At one point during the retreat, Rocko was speaking to a group of us, and one by one, people asked Rocko questions about their lives. He would close his eyes and appear to see into the future. Believing he might tell me something I needed to hear, I finally got up the courage to raise my hand, salivating at the idea of receiving insight about the direction my life was going so I didn't have to feel so lost all the time.

But for no apparent reason, when Rocko saw my hand raised, he snapped, "Jan, you're a spiritual pain in the ass!"

His words stung, and I shrank into my seat. I looked over at Joel and he put his arm around me; at least I wasn't alone. But even after Rocko's harsh comment in front of the whole group, my obsession for him continued.

ONE DAY, MONTHS AFTER THAT RETREAT, ROCKO ASKED IF I would like to go to San Jose and help him with a workshop. He'd never explained why he'd lashed out at me, and I never had the courage to ask, so I remained just as devoted and en-amored with him as ever.

"Yes," I said eagerly. "I would love to go."

When I told Joel about it, all he said was, "Have a good time." But the tinge of sarcasm in his voice didn't escape me.

Why isn't he fighting for me? I wondered. *Doesn't he care? He must know how I feel about Rocko.*

But Joel didn't fight for me to stay, so off I went.

I was glad to be going alone with Rocko, but I was plagued with questions about what this meant for our relationship. I had no idea if he expected us to share a room or if he was in-terested in pursuing a romatic relationship with me. I didn't know if he felt the same chemistry I did, but I assumed he must—it was too powerful to be ignored.

When we got to the hotel in San Jose, Rocko checked us in and we took our luggage to our room—*our* room. I was so ecstatic to finally have my time alone with him that I could barely contain the surges I felt throughout my body.

The workshop followed the usual pattern: the participants were intrigued and the women vied for Rocko's attention. They hung around after the workshop was over, and then a few of us went out for drinks. I watched Rocko for signs that it was time to leave, and at last, he nodded to me.

On our way back to the hotel we talked casually about the

people in the workshop. Then, after we entered our room, I lay down on one bed as Rocko plunked himself down on the other, seemingly exhausted. He then proceeded to call his wife and several other women I suspected he had been romantically linked to.

How skilled he was at keeping me on the edge.

It seemed like hours before he hung up the phone, after which he told me his neck was bothering him.

No wonder, with all those phone calls.

I couldn't stand it anymore. I got up and went over to his bed, climbed in next to him, and pressed my body against his back. I began massaging his neck, and our breathing became rhythmic as I worked out the knots. Finally, he turned his body toward me and kissed me.

The endless orgasms I had already experienced by simply being in his presence every day left me hungry for more. But, as things heated up, I soon learned that Rocko had nothing to give.

He couldn't perform in bed.

But in true Jan fashion, instead of recognizing that the lack of performance was Rocko's issue, I worried that something was dreadfully wrong with me. I didn't ask him about it, and he didn't offer an explanation, so I embarked on a new focus: I turned into more of a Rocko groupie than ever before, determined to learn everything I could to improve myself.

More than anything, I still wanted to be free, yet here I was attaching myself to this man who was quite possibly stringing me along. Never mind that Joel was still my husband, though he was living our open marriage with his own careless abandon, I was sure.

In the midst of my Rocko frenzy, we were talking about an upcoming event one day when I asked Rocko a simple question. Instead of answering me, he turned sharply to face me and blurted out, "Jan, do you realize how annoying you are?"

Feeling chastised the way I had when he'd snapped at me in front of everyone at the retreat, I was taken aback.

He continued, "Questions, questions, questions all the time. You're absurd. Just go out and do what you want. You don't need anyone to help you get what you want."

His words stopped me in my tracks. I felt a pain directly in the center of my heart, as if he had stabbed me. I knew he was speaking the truth, but I was clueless as to how to strike out on my own. Even though I wanted to live independently, I wasn't ready to take responsibility for my life.

Realizing then that Rocko had given me all he could, I heard a voice call to me from within.

"Jan, I'm over here. Can't you see me? Rocko's not your savior. I am. I'm the part of you that can fulfill all your dreams. Drop him and surrender to me. I will take you where you want to go."

The words didn't make sense to me at the time, so I ignored the voice. I wanted a quick fix.

But if not Rocko, then who?

Joel?

No, I was aware at that point that it wasn't going to be him either. I knew in my heart that our marriage was over. Feeling lost and alone, I seemed to know myself less than I did not only before I got married, but also before I met Rocko.

I hated to admit it—and I was scared out of my mind—but it was time to move on.

9

THE GROUP

*D*ISHES, *LAUNDRY, FILING, UNFINISHED LETTERS* ... *how can I get it all done? I can see my work piled up all around me, but the light is dimming. I struggle to see, until I realize my eyes are closed. The harder I fight to open them, the darker it gets. Why am I working in complete darkness, without any of the tools I need? I have to get this all done. Why is this happening to me? In the distance I hear a hum. I focus in on the sound, and it turns into a ringing.*

I woke with a start and fumbled to answer the phone.

"Hi, Jan. How are you?"

I sat up abruptly as his voice awakened that vulnerable place inside me.

"Hi, Joel."

Feeling a mixture of excitement and irritation, I didn't know what to say. It was 1976, and Joel and I had agreed to separate after toying with the idea for about a year. It was time for me to move on and I knew I didn't want to stay with Joel forever, so I agreed to move in with a friend who needed a roommate. When I moved out, Joel and I agreed not to have contact with each other for three months so we could each get on with our lives. It had only been a couple of weeks, and Joel was not honoring our agreement.

I was twenty-eight years old. Though I had a steady job in

a small office, I barely made enough money to take care of myself. I didn't like the job, but ready for my independence, come what may, it would do for the moment.

But despite my sense of having done the right thing in splitting with Joel, it had been difficult to leave him. I still loved my soldier boy and believed I always would. The day I moved out, he was right there with me, helping me cart my things away. I struggled the entire time to hold back the sobbing that was rising from within me.

When I told my family that Joel and I were splitting up, they were shocked. To them, we were the perfect couple. They had no idea that the babies they were expecting were never going to come.

As sad as Joel seemed too, I noticed him giving my new roommate Rachel a lot of attention. Being cute and female, she was irresistible to him.

How many signs do I need to prove that moving on is good for both of us?

"Why are you calling so late?" I said, obviously irritated.

"I was thinking about you, and I wanted to hear your voice."

Muffled music and voices echoing in the background told me he was at a bar, and probably drunk.

"Can I come over, Kitten? I miss you."

My mind screamed, *No, definitely not!* But what I said was, "Sure. I'll leave the door unlocked for you."

Rachel had gone to visit her parents for the weekend, so Joel and I would be alone. In complete conflict with myself, I thought maybe I could handle one night with him, that perhaps he was still in love with me. Unable to even feel my body, I felt cloaked in an uncomfortable anxiety, afraid to move a muscle, waiting for the door to open. I was aware of every sound that interrupted the stillness of the night—a siren from an ambulance racing to someone's aid, the steady hum of the refrigerator, and even my heart jumping erratically with apprehension and excitement. Joel was like home to me, and there was a part of me that was not yet willing to let go.

I heard the door open and close quietly, and then Joel's footsteps as he followed the light into my bedroom. He stood beside my bed and took off his clothes. Reeking of liquor and stale smoke, he slurred, "Hi, Kitten."

His words used to make me melt, but now they made me feel uneasy. Joel clearly wanted sex, but I wanted to believe that he desired more than that. I had hoped he'd come because he wanted to change, to talk to me honestly about his feelings, but all I was getting was the same tired routine.

He climbed into bed beside me and began making the usual moves intended to turn me on. But where was the talk? Where was the change? I didn't want the same old Joel. When he put his arms around me and nibbled at my ear, I instinctively turned away. He didn't seem to notice. Instead he began moving his pelvis rhythmically against my body as I slid farther away.

"I want to sleep," I said.

"Okay," he said, exasperated.

He got up and went into the kitchen, and I heard the refrigerator door open and slam shut. I knew he was angry, but I couldn't help myself. Nothing had changed.

Awhile later, he came back to bed, but I pretended to be asleep.

As usual, we lay next to each other, separate and alone. I couldn't stop myself from giving him mixed messages.

Don't leave me. Don't come near me.

THE NEXT MORNING, JOEL GOT UP EARLY.

"Jan, you need to get some help," he said as he left.

His words cut fresh wounds into my heart. Feeling more

alone and misunderstood than ever before, I curled up in bed, holding myself. *Maybe he's right. Maybe I do need help.*

I decided to call Joel's sister, Evelyn. In the past, she had told me about a therapy group she was in, and I hoped it would be okay with her if I joined.

"Sure. No problem," she said when I called and asked about the group.

Evelyn was smart, funny, beautiful, and not afraid to speak her mind; in fact, she intimidated me. Like the rest of Joel's family, I never knew when to take her seriously or when she was teasing. At the same time I felt powerless around her, I also wanted to be more like her—bold and fearless.

She had good things to say about the therapy group, and I trusted her judgment. The group was facilitated by two therapists in their forties—Seth and Ed—who were working under another therapist's license, as they were both fairly new to the profession and still accumulating hours toward their own accreditations. Evelyn spoke highly of them, especially Ed. She said he was one of the most interesting and exciting men she had ever met. An odd description of a therapist, I thought, but I was curious so I agreed to come.

The following Sunday, I prepared for my first meeting with the group. Being uncomfortable with my body, I spent a ridiculous amount of time choosing the right thing to wear; I dreaded having some man notice me and want something from me, so what I wore couldn't be too revealing, but I also wanted to feel good in it. Was that too much to ask? But nothing I put on seemed to fit right and the chatter in my head was hostile.

My butt looks big in these jeans.

I can't wear this blouse. It's too sheer. Someone might see my breasts.

These pants are too baggy.

I'm short.

I'm not attractive.

I'll never get what I want.

In the end, I put on an old pair of jeans and a T-shirt and pulled my hair back in a ponytail.

I arrived at the two-story business complex right on time. It had been built to look like a small Spanish villa, but sandwiched between an auto shop and an abandoned gas station, it lacked ambiance. A group of people stood on the balcony, talking jovially and laughing. I watched as a thin, beautiful woman wearing a tight-fitting, brightly colored top, shorts that hugged her tiny, well-formed butt, and cute white sandals that showed off her shapely legs walked toward them. I felt like a slob in comparison. I considered starting up the car and going back home.

But despite feeling completely out of place, I was curious to see how this group might help me deal with my insecurities. I was conscious of my habit of comparing myself to others and was determined to find out what was wrong with me—and how to fix it.

I waited until everyone was inside, and then I got out of my car and found the room, hoping I wouldn't have to mingle. Small and cold, the meeting space smelled of stale smoke and coffee. A circle of gray metal folding chairs punctuated the center of the room, and I sat down in one nearest the door. Their eyes on me were unnerving.

"Hi," I said, wishing the session would start soon so I didn't have to socialize. *If only I could be invisible right now.*

The pretty woman in the bright colored top was sitting to my left and introduced herself as Lisa. "I understand if you're nervous," she whispered.

I smiled awkwardly.

"It's very confrontational," she said, "but you can trust these people."

To my right, a good-looking man wearing a fitted shirt and tight jeans introduced himself as Russell. "Don't worry," he said jokingly, "I'll beat up anyone who's not nice to you. I'm glad you're here."

A woman with kind eyes sitting next to Russell leaned over and said, "Hi, I'm Lori. It's nice to meet you."

Another woman was busy making sure everything was in order in the room. Russell told me her name was Beth.

Everyone seems nice so far.

Evelyn, the only person I knew, was the last to arrive. Entering from an office in the back, she looked at me and smiled. In most of my past interactions with her, I'd felt like she was mocking me, but this smile seemed genuine. When she greeted me, though, her tone was a little too formal, like she didn't really know me.

"Hi, Jan," she said, "I'm glad you could make it."

I imagined the members knew that Evelyn and I were sisters-in law. She had been in the group for a while, and I assumed she would have mentioned her brother and his wife at some point. It might not have mattered, but I didn't want to hide that we knew each other.

The two therapists then made their entrance from that same office door Evelyn had come through, giving the air that they were obviously older and wiser and this was their group.

I noticed Seth right away. Tall, with a commanding presence, he looked at me with deep, mysterious brown eyes. I knew then I had come to the right place. I had never seen anyone like him—his frizzy gray hair stuck out wildly all over his head, and he was barefoot, wore overalls, and didn't seem to care what people thought of him. He had a bit of a potbelly, and his skin was pockmarked, but he was clearly comfortable with himself. Despite his sloppy appearance, he seemed wise, sensitive, and intelligent.

Ed was shorter and rounder than Seth, clad in a T-shirt, shorts, and sandals that looked like they had been with him for a while. As he laughed heartily at something Evelyn said to him, I couldn't help noticing that they seemed flirtatious and quite taken with each other.

It would be nice to have a male friend like that, I thought, *but how close are they? Does Evelyn's husband know about this?*

When Beth walked over and closed the door, it creaked shut like in a scary movie, followed by an eerie silence.

Seth and Ed introduced themselves as the leaders of the group. Then Seth began speaking in a gentle, deep, soothing voice—he had that kind of sexy drawl that in a different situation might have turned me on. He focused directly on me, his intensity cutting through me like a laser. I shifted uncomfortably, not wanting to be the center of attention, but I supposed I was the only newcomer.

"Jan, this group is very serious and committed," he said. "We work hard and we don't back down. We get in each other's faces when we have to. I don't want to scare you away, but that's how this group works."

I looked around and saw the others nodding and listening intently. A couple of them watched me closely to see how I was responding.

"When you're in the hot seat," he continued, "we expect you to be honest and to let us be honest with you."

I glanced at Evelyn, hoping she would shoot me a look or crack a joke like she usually did to break the intense vibe in the room. But she didn't. She merely smiled at me as if she knew something I didn't, and then quickly glanced away.

"Also," Seth added, "nothing that happens in this room is to be shared with anyone outside of this room. Everything we discuss is confidential. We want to keep this a safe place to express ourselves so we can grow. Will you agree to this?"

"Yes," I said emphatically. I had no idea what I was getting myself into, but I felt ready to jump in.

Seth asked me to tell everyone why I decided to join the group. I was nervous, but the fact that I didn't actually know these people, aside from Evelyn, was also strangely comforting.

"I'm not sure why I'm here," I said, my voice tentative and shaky. "I'm unhappy with my life ... and my husband told me I needed some help. I think it's really him who needs the help, but he won't admit it."

I avoided Evelyn's eyes and paused for a moment, thinking about how crazy Joel acted sometimes and how calm I had always been. I felt like I was betraying him by saying that he needed help and wondered if Evelyn was going to tell him.

So what? I reasoned. *He hurt me, and I'm not going to let that go on any longer.*

My eyes briefly met Russell's, whom I instinctively felt wouldn't harm me.

I continued, "My husband wants a divorce. I still love him, but it's not working. I don't know what to do. He wants to keep seeing me and being my friend. I would like to be able to do that too, but it hurts too much." I paused again, looking down at the floor. "And then I fell in love with someone else, but he doesn't respect me. I can't seem to stay away from him, so I guess I'm kind of lost right now."

In that moment I flashed back to something that had happened to me when I was a little girl, at the grocery store with Mom. I had been tugging on her skirt, crying to be picked up. But when I looked up, it wasn't my mom; it was another random woman in the store.

As I sat there in that circle at group therapy, I felt momentarily lost, like that day in the store. I was anxious to find the something that was missing in my life. But I didn't know how to find it, or even what it was I was looking for.

Having given my little sob story, Seth asked the group to introduce themselves to me and express how they were feeling about my being there.

Lori softly said, "I'm afraid you'll make fun of me and judge me before you get a chance to know me."

Wow! They cut right to the chase.

Evelyn chimed in that she was glad I was there because it would give her a chance to get to know me better. Then she added, "I don't trust you, Jan. I never have. You're not honest about your feelings, and it makes me angry."

What is she talking about? I've always gone out of my way to be nice to her.

Russell said he was delighted to have me join the group. "Things have been getting a little stale. I hope you'll stir things up, but I also hope you'll be truly honest with us about how you're feeling."

Beth said she would rather not have another person join the group at this time because she was happy with the way it was going, and she didn't want to have to tell her story all over again to someone new. "But since you're here," she said, "I just hope you'll be as forthright as everyone else and stay in the game. I hope you won't try to hide. Hiding doesn't work here. If you try to hide, we'll be on you."

My eyes widened.

"Don't even try it," she said. "You'll be wasting our time."

Why does she think I'm going to hide?

Lisa said, "I'm glad you're here. I sense a connection with you, and I think we could be friends."

So, there it was: true feelings out on the table. These people expected me to be myself, and I was about to learn that being myself was a tall order. I was used to blending in, trying to please everyone at all costs, and I could see that was not going to work here.

The session then began in earnest. I listened as the others talked, as their words and emotions seemed to flow easily— likely, I assumed, because they all knew one another.

Being the only "outsider" there, I was reminded of high school and the cliques I never fit into. Drifting into a fog, I could hear their voices as they shared, but I couldn't relate to what they were saying.

Lori voiced her frustration at being overweight and feeling unattractive. I snapped out of my haze as she burst into tears, complaining that she had tried everything to lose the extra pounds but that nothing was working.

"Maybe you think you're safer and less attractive in the heavy body you have now," Ed suggested. "Maybe it's keeping you from being open to intimacy with a man."

Wow, that's harsh, I thought. *But really, how hard is it to lose the weight?*

After everyone shared, it was finally my turn.

"Jan, what are you feeling right now?" Seth asked.

His intensity made me cringe. Everyone stared at me. My mind raced, my body went numb, and my hands grew clammy. They wanted an honest answer—and I wanted to give them one, but I was paralyzed with fear. I was used to letting others get emotional while remaining the steady one. That had been my job in the family. I wasn't used to being listened to, and I certainly wasn't accustomed to telling people how I really felt.

My thoughts suddenly took me out of the situation, thinking of everything but the question at hand.

What am I going to have for dinner? Where is Joel? Is he with a woman? Did I send that package out at work?

Not wanting to give the wrong answers or make a fool of myself, I felt stupid, ashamed, and a little resentful that they were putting so much pressure on me. As I wished I could melt away and go back to observing, I looked up and noticed a loose ceiling tile. I wondered what would happen if it fell on me at that moment.

"I don't know," I said, my voice a faint quiver.

"That's not acceptable," Seth rebuffed. "I think you do know."

The rest of the group agreed. A few of them nodded and said out loud that they wanted to know how I was feeling. They didn't trust my passive silence.

My face flushed. "I'm sorry."

Ed spoke then. "Jan, I think you're sitting here listening and judging us all, but you're not willing to tell us how you feel because you're afraid we won't like what you have to say."

They can read that from my face? Does he know what I'm thinking about Lori? Does he know I think he's fat too? Does he know I think I'm too short? Does he know I judge myself more harshly than anyone else? Do I know that?

I felt trapped in my skin, busted at my own game.

As Ed sat up in his chair and spoke to me with a firm voice, similar to my father's, I felt like I was being punished once again.

"You may think it's easy for the rest of us to solve our problems, but what about *your* problems? It's easy to judge, but how is your self-doubt any different than what Lori is feeling about her weight problems?"

The room was closing in on me, and I looked at the door. I could run out of there and forget this had ever happened. But I knew that wasn't the answer.

I stewed over Ed as he sat there silently, seeming to know me so well already while my judgments were running rampant.

Who does he think he is? That stupid cowlick in his hair is driving me crazy.

Evelyn's a bitch. She acts like she's better than everyone, or, as Joel would say, "like her shit don't stink." But he probably wouldn't say that about his own sister, even though it's true. And she's obviously flirting with Ed, which is distracting. She's married with children. What kind of dangerous game is she playing?

Beth thinks she knows what's best for everyone. She didn't even want me in the group. I don't need that woman telling me what I should and shouldn't do, thank you very much.

Russell is Russell. I kind of like him. He doesn't feel threatening, at least not right now.

Lisa is clueless. Why is she staying with a man who treats her so badly? Maybe it's because she has such low self-esteem. Why can't she just see what she's doing to herself and get out of the situation?

Seth is arrogant and aloof. He acts like he knows something we don't.

But I couldn't say any of this if I wanted them to like me. Or could I?

I burst into tears. "I'm so sorry," I whimpered. "Ed's right. I'm sitting here thinking all these bad things about all of you."

"Let's hear it," said Beth.

I had no choice. It was either be honest and risk telling the truth, or be crushed once again.

The words spilled out of me like a volcanic eruption.

"Ed, I think you like to see people suffer. You find their weakness and then you go for the jugular. Lori, I'm sorry you're fat, but I wish you'd not complain so much about it and just lose the weight already. I hate being small. Lisa, why do you act like such a victim? Beth, I wish you would stop being so authoritative. You're not our mother! Evelyn, you've always thought you were better than me. You've been mean to me as long as I've known you. Russell, I feel good about you. And Seth ... I hate you for intimidating me. There, I said it!"

I couldn't believe what I had just expressed out loud—or how good it felt. My satisfaction didn't last long, though. I immediately feared I'd now be thrown out of the group.

I had come here to take a risk, but now they knew what a

bitch I could be. And I was forced to admit that "nice" was just a game I played to avoid telling the scary truth. I couldn't be a nice girl and a bitch at the same time. One of these sides would have to go. Or was it that simple?

They sat there for a moment, not saying anything. I didn't know how to interpret their silence, but I breathed a quiet sigh of relief when I realized they weren't yelling back at me. I had taken a big step with that confession, and I suddenly realized that they were all looking at me as if I had done something valiant. I had been on the hot seat, and apparently, I passed. I felt bad for the things I said, but I had told the truth without holding back.

Denial is powerful, and I'd always been good at it, but I thought it was everyone else who was in denial. Now that the others in the group knew the other side of me, I knew I was going to be held accountable from here on out, to take responsibility for conquering my demons.

But how?

We all moved on, and for the rest of the session, I listened and felt sincere compassion for these people who were willing to be truthful. I didn't know what to expect for the future, but for my first time, it felt good.

I drove home that night completely exhausted, but knowing I'd be back the following week.

RIGHT BEFORE I FELL ASLEEP, JOEL CALLED ME TO SAY hello and see how I was doing, making me wonder how much he sincerely still cared about me.

I lingered on the phone longer than I wanted to, waiting for him to end the conversation. After he said good-bye, I fell asleep easily. We had been separated for months now, and I was beginning to feel more confident about moving on.

I continued to meet with the group on a regular basis, but despite feeling a bit more comfortable around them, I still froze whenever they asked me how I felt. Finding a way to open up fully was like trying to squeeze juice out of a rock. Somewhere inside, unconsciously, I was determined to stay shut down.

Then Seth suggested private sessions.

⌘

10

PRIVATE SESSIONS

*M*Y FIRST APPOINTMENT WITH SETH WAS AFTER work one Tuesday. It was pouring rain, and traffic was jammed. I kept checking the rearview mirror to make sure my hair was in place and I looked presentable, as I watched the clock tick toward our meeting time.

When I arrived half an hour late, the note on the door read, "In session. Please wait." I was too wired to relax, and now I felt angry and entitled.

How dare he keep me waiting after I stressed myself out to get here?

At last the door opened slightly, and I saw Seth hugging an attractive woman. As she walked out, I noticed that her hair was tousled and she looked like she had been crying.

What was I getting myself into?

Seth excused himself, saying he'd be right back. Then, he returned and led me into his office. As I walked past the coffee area, I noticed two empty wine glasses and caught a whiff of perfume like my aunt used to wear, causing me to wonder how close Seth was to that woman. I knew it was none of my business, but I was curious nonetheless.

Not knowing what to expect, I felt anxious about going

into his office with him. As he closed the door, I brushed my hair behind my ears and straightened my clothes.

It was a small room, barely large enough for the two chairs that faced each other and a bookcase filled with works on psychology and the occult. Seth's big leather chair squeaked when he sat down; mine was worn, with wing-like arms covered in new fabric. It looked like something out of my parents' house.

"Jan, tell me, how are you feeling?" he began. "It's just you and me in this room. There's nothing to be afraid of."

But there *was* something to be afraid of. I was alone in a room with a man who wanted me to tell him how I was feeling. I wasn't sure how I was feeling, and even after having group therapy sessions with Seth, I still didn't trust him. Despite the scent of his cologne that reminded me of how much I wanted to be held by a strong, loving man, I felt trapped. I knew that if I didn't say something soon, I would begin to feel incredibly stupid.

"I'm nervous," I said.

"Why are you nervous?" Seth spoke with that deep, sexy drawl I was becoming addicted to.

"Because I don't know what to say."

"Jan, look at me. You always avoid my eyes."

Oh, no. If I look into his eyes, he'll know I'm attracted to him, and then I'll be in real trouble.

I sighed deeply and did as he asked.

"Jan, you can trust me. I'm not going to hurt you."

I thought I saw compassion and depth in him, yet I remembered how compassionate and loving Dad had looked sometimes, and how he would betray me. I had to be on guard all the time for fear of being put down, made fun of, punished, or exploited. Nothing I did was ever good enough.

"Jan, I'm not Joel, or any of the other men in your life,"

said Seth. "And I'm not your father either. I'm your therapist, and I'm here to help you."

How does he know I'm comparing him to Dad?

I looked away quickly and noticed a small clock on a table in the back of the room.

"Jan, don't worry about the time," he said. "My next client is going to be late, so let's keep going."

He was relentless, and I was stubborn. Something would have to give.

I looked into his eyes and said, "Okay. I'm so confused. I don't know what I'm doing with my life."

"And what are you feeling now?"

"Angry. I want you to leave me alone."

"Do you really want to be alone?"

"No."

"Who are you angry with?"

"Joel."

"So it's not me you're angry with, is it?"

"No."

At that moment, he made me realize that I was indeed confused, that I was ready for therapy. It was time to start looking at my life in depth, and I had found the help I needed.

At the end of our session, Seth hugged me. It was a gentle and loving embrace, and my body stirred as it hadn't in months.

SOON AFTER I BEGAN MEETING ONE-ON-ONE WITH SETH, I got a call at work.

"Hi, Jan. How are you?"

Joel.

My heart leapt, and I sat up straight. I still felt that tingle in my body upon hearing his voice.

"Listen, Jan, I have our tax refund and I need you to sign it so I can pay some final bills. Will you be home tonight?"

"Well," I said, "I have a therapy appointment after work, but I guess you can stop by later."

Maybe he'll come over and stay the night with me, and it'll be just like old times. How dare he sound so confident and sexy?

I was weak, and still convinced that I needed him. What was I thinking?

That evening I arrived at Seth's office on the dot, and this time he was ready to see me. I walked in sad, my head hanging.

"What's going on with you tonight, Jan?"

"Joel called me. He wants to come over and have me endorse our tax refund so he can cash it and pay some of our outstanding bills. It's okay with me because we don't have much left between us and it will be good to clear it up. But every time I see him, I go back to wanting him to take care of me."

"Jan, why does he need to come over to your place to have you endorse the check?"

It was a good question.

"I don't know," I said. "He wants to come over, I guess."

"Why don't you meet him somewhere, and you can sign the check and be done with it?"

"I don't know if he'll go along with that."

"Jan, look at me. I want you to do something that's probably going to be uncomfortable for you. Joel telling you he wants to come over is out and out manipulation. If he wants a divorce, then it's time for you to take care of business and get on with your life."

"But I'm scared to tell him not to come over."

"And why is that?"

"I don't know. I can't help myself. I just do everything he wants me to do."

"Is this making you happy?"

"No. Definitely not."

"Okay," Seth said, leaning toward me, "are you willing to trust me and try something different?"

"Okay."

"Are you sure?"

"Yes, I'm sure. I'm tired of being manipulated, and I'm tired of the way things are. So ... yes."

"Then this is what I want you to do. I want you to call Joel and tell him that you would prefer to meet him in a neutral place to sign the papers."

"I'm not sure he'll like that."

"Do you want to change?"

"Yes, I do."

"Then call him. If you want, I'll sit right here while you do it."

I hesitated, but I knew Seth was right. "Okay."

I took a couple of deep breaths and called Joel. When he answered, I was direct. "Joel, I was wondering if we could meet somewhere else tonight, other than my place."

"Why?"

"I just think it would be better."

"Okay, how about that place near your apartment? We can have a drink."

"A drink?" I looked at Seth. He shook his head.

"No, Joel. I don't really want a drink. Why don't we meet in the shopping center parking lot at nine o'clock, near the main street there?"

"Okay," he said. "I'll see you then."

I could tell he was annoyed.

It was only seven-thirty, so I still had time to work this through with Seth.

"Joel is probably not going to be happy about your abruptness," Seth said. "He's not used to that. He's used to being in control. So here's what I want you to do. Meet him at nine, endorse the check, and tell him good-bye. Tell him you have to be someplace. I know this will be difficult for you. He's going to want to talk you into being with him, but you have to stick to your plan."

I furrowed my brow as he spelled out the plan.

"I'll tell you what. Come back here right after you meet with him, and we'll talk about it. That way, you'll actually have somewhere to be."

"Okay," I agreed, feeling a touch of newfound confidence ... for now.

I left Seth's office at eight-thirty and drove to the parking lot, arriving close to nine. I waited twenty minutes before Joel drove up. After getting out of his car, he walked over and leaned down to my window.

"Hi, Kitten. It's good to see you."

Hearing him call me Kitten always melted my heart. But I was committed to my plan.

"Hi, Joel. Is that the check?"

"Yeah. Let me get in the car so you can sign it."

"No, that's okay. I'll just sign it and be on my way."

Joel stood there while I looked at the check, then turned it over and signed it. I knew he wasn't going to go away easily.

"Okay, thanks, Joel." I handed it back to him. "I'll see you."

"What's your hurry?"

"I have someplace to be."

"Oh, come on, Jan. Let's go have a drink."

Conflicted, a part of me wanted to go with him, but a bigger part of me didn't.

Remembering Seth's instructions, I recognized that I was doing something I wasn't used to, and that I truly did have a place to be, which made me feel excited about going back to see Seth.

"I'm sorry, Joel. I really have to go."

"Where are you going? Where do you have to be at this time of night?"

"I just have to be somewhere. Good-bye."

I rolled up the window and started the engine, doing my best to ignore Joel's yelling and banging on the window. He wasn't getting his way, and he was angry that I wasn't being my usual, wimpy self. As I pulled out of the parking lot and drove away, I couldn't help feeling bad about leaving him like that.

But Seth was right. Changing my behavior did make a difference. I took it as a wake-up call, a loud signal showing me just how dependent I had been, afraid to rock the boat and trigger Joel's anger.

As difficult as it was to cut my meeting with Joel short, I believed Seth was someone who honestly cared about me and wanted the best for me. When I got back to his office, he welcomed me with a big hug. We sat down to talk, and I thanked him for showing me that I could be different. I also told him I was afraid of how Joel might respond to me in the future because of this incident. He said I shouldn't worry, that I could always come and talk to him about it.

I knew I needed to find my own autonomy, but at the same time, I was drawn to Seth and relished the idea of him taking care of me. I couldn't wait to see him again.

MY SESSIONS WITH SETH BECAME MY LIFELINE, AND I became quite comfortable with him. Convinced that he would help me heal my past and move forward in my life, we discussed the mysteries of life and relationships. Not only were our views compatible, but his intelligence and wisdom stimulated me, and I began to discover those qualities in myself as well. He was a good listener, encouraging me to question my beliefs and explore new possibilities—and he made me feel like I was the only one he cared about.

When I shared with Seth about growing up in my family, and about how overwhelming it had been to carry so much responsibility, he was sincerely compassionate. As I finally explored getting to the bottom of some foundational issues in my life, Seth let me talk on and on about my past. As I expressed my feelings and he didn't berate me for them, I grew to trust him.

During one particular session, Seth's soft, caring voice pushed me over the edge when he asked me how I was feeling.

"Ashamed. And abandoned," I said, bursting into tears.

Seth came over and sat with me, rocking me in his arms.

"It's okay, Jan. I'm here now. I won't ever abandon you. You're safe with me. You're a very special woman and I want to help you. What your parents did was not your fault. You were just a child. You didn't know any better."

Realizing what I had been missing all my life, and believing Seth didn't treat any of his other patients with such tenderness, I cried like a baby in his arms.

What a relief, I thought, safe in his embrace. *I am not responsible for taking care of my family. Maybe I can have a life now.*

⁓⧓⁓

11

STRANGE DEVELOPMENTS

$\mathcal{I}$ SAW SETH PRIVATELY ONCE A WEEK. AFTER FINDING a man who provided me with a safe harbor, it didn't take me long to get attached to him.

One day, after a few months of sessions, I arrived at his office for a morning appointment and found a note that read, "Gone to play. Please call and reschedule."

Who is he playing with? I wondered.

He had told me I was special, and I believed him. I knew he spent time with several women in the group, but he had assured me that I was different.

I wanted to be open and accepting, and I reminded myself that Seth was my therapist and that he was supposed to be teaching me how to be in a healthy relationship. Letting go was healthy; attaching myself to him was not.

When I called to reschedule my appointment, I resisted asking whom he had spent the day with. Seth suggested I come for my regular appointment the following week.

I was still having trouble resolving my ambivalence about Joel, and it was becoming increasingly difficult for me to get through the day at work without feeling pain in my heart over our split. I missed him a lot. And I still thought of Rocko and desired to feel the surrender I had experienced with him.

One day, out of the blue, Joel's sister Evelyn showed up at my workplace. She had a friend with her, but she didn't bother to introduce us. They merely exchanged looks and giggled as Evelyn handed me an envelope.

"What's this?" I asked.

I saw my name on an official-looking envelope, but before I had a chance to open it, they dashed out. When I did, my knees went weak and I fell back into my chair.

I had just been served with divorce papers. I knew they would show up one day, but from his sister?

Awhile back, when Joel had come over and discussed the possibility of divorce, I told him I couldn't conceive of it going that far. Joel had begun dating someone else, but I simply wasn't ready for such finality. Despite my awareness that Joel and I weren't meant to be together, I sat for a long time after he left that day, doubled over in pain, feeling like my insides were being torn apart.

I went home early that day; I had lost my husband, and I was forced to admit that what I had thought of as a friendship with his sister was over as well. I drove to my therapy appointment with tears streaming down my face and told Seth what had happened.

"I'm sorry, Jan," he said. "You don't deserve to be treated that way."

"She's a bitch, Seth. She's such a bitch. I thought we were friends. How could she do this to me?"

"It's okay, Jan. Let your anger out."

He set up some pillows and handed me a plastic bat, and I began pounding them, harder and faster, out of control. First I beat up Evelyn, then Joel, then Rocko, then my dad.

"Keep going, Jan. Yes. Yes. Get it all out."

I had no idea I had that much anger inside of me. I pounded and yelled until I was spent and my voice went hoarse. Exhausted, I collapsed on the floor.

Seth gently stroked my face. "It's okay, Jan. You are loved. The anger is good."

Seeing how drained I was, Seth suggested I lie down. I didn't object when he lay beside me, comforting me until I fell asleep. When I woke up in the middle of the night, he was still lying beside me, snoring peacefully. I snuggled closer to him, and he stirred and kissed me on the forehead. My body craved more, though; I wanted him to make love to me, but we both fell back to sleep. When we awoke again at dawn, I got up in time to go home, grab a shower, and go to work. But my body was still vibrating from spending the night in Seth's arms.

My attachment to Seth deepened, and I wanted to be with him as often as possible. Technically we were still therapist and client, but I didn't see it that way anymore. He had become the most important man in my life.

One day, while having lunch with Christine, I shared my excitement about how well my therapy was going and how much I enjoyed Seth.

"Jan, I don't want to burst your bubble or anything," she said dryly, "but Seth is your therapist. Don't you think it's a little strange that he lets you spend the night with him?"

"No, you don't understand. That's how Seth does therapy. He believes in getting emotionally involved with his clients to help heal relationship issues. And it's working. I'm learning how to be in a relationship," I insisted.

"Okay, but have you thought about the fact that if he does this with you, he may be doing it with other clients too? It's probably not a good idea to get too attached to him. He's your therapist. There are rules about that, you know."

She continued to insist I be cautious and careful, while I tensed up inside and wanted to lash out at her.

"Oh, don't worry," I said defensively. "It's different with me. He doesn't spend the night with anyone else. I'm always the last appointment of the day, so it works out great. Besides, I think the relationship is progressing beyond therapy."

"How do you know he doesn't spend the night with his other clients?" Christine asked suspiciously.

"Oh, come on. He told me I was special."

"Okay, Jan, but as your friend, I'm really concerned about you."

"Then as my friend, why don't you trust me? I've already told you how it is. I know what's going on. He makes me feel good." I paused a moment to reflect, then said, "And I think I might be falling in love with him."

Christine shot me a disapproving look.

Irritated, I rolled my eyes and changed the subject. It was obvious to me that she didn't understand. I ignored the part of me that knew she had valid concerns and left lunch angry with Christine for trying to control me.

Once again, my desire to be loved by a man no matter what trumped reason.

I ARRIVED AT SETH'S OFFICE ONE EVENING TO FIND THAT he wasn't ready for me at my usual appointment time.

"Make yourself comfortable, Jan. I'll be right with you," he said, disappearing into the adjoining bathroom.

Seth and Ed had moved into a more spacious office. The therapy rooms and waiting room were newly furnished, and there was a full bathroom, complete with a shower.

The room was quiet, except for Neil Diamond songs playing softly on the stereo. When I heard the sound of the shower, I imagined the water beating down on Seth's naked body.

Seth eventually emerged from the now steamy bathroom wrapped in a towel that barely covered the lower part of his body, like this was a perfectly natural thing to do. He had told me he was no longer living with his girlfriend, and I felt like he must be especially comfortable with me, possibly even decided that I was the one, which excited me and made me nervous at the same time.

"Relax, Jan," he said. "You can take a shower too, if you want. Don't worry about putting your clothes back on. It's much freer this way."

Really?

My legs trembled and my heart beat so fast I thought it was going to jump out of my body. I'd always been shy and inhibited. Maybe this would help liberate me.

As I thought of how big and powerful he was, and how I wanted him to take me into his arms, I didn't stop to think. I was riding too high on desire to do that. But then a crazy conversation began in my head.

Jan, what do you think you're doing? He's your therapist. This will change everything.

I don't care. I've waited for this moment for a long time, and I'm going for it.

It's not worth it.

I don't care. I want him. I'll show him that I'm the best, and I'll forget about how unattractive I feel. He'll make it all better. I know he will.

As I stood there wondering if I should take him up on the shower, Seth's towel slipped off and fell to the floor. He made no move to cover himself, standing in front of me, naked, with a confident smile on his face. Gathering some pillows from the sofa, he brought them over, covered them with the towel, and sat down on the floor.

"I'll wait here while you take a shower," he said, making the decision for me.

I enjoyed showering, excitedly appreciating my nakedness in a way I never had before. I emerged refreshed and filled with anticipation, clutching a towel tightly around me. I noticed that Seth had placed lit candles around the room. The Neil Diamond music, so familiar and soothing to me, set the stage perfectly for a romantic evening.

"Come over here, Jan. You have a beautiful body. You should never be ashamed of it."

I walked over and lay down beside him. He began touching my body, and I shivered as my towel slipped to the floor.

He was right: I shouldn't be ashamed of my body. Feeling free and open at last, I breathed more deeply with each touch, and my body began to move in ways I had never experienced before, stretching and contracting as I moaned with pleasure. It was the connection I had always wanted, and this man was finally giving it to me. We were on the floor for hours, drifting in and out of sleep, kissing and making out.

I woke early in the morning before he did. When I crawled on top of him, he woke up and kissed me. I wanted to consummate our relationship, but I also wanted to keep my therapist.

Pulling me to him, Seth kissed me lightly on the lips, rolled me over, and then got up. That was my cue to leave. My session was over.

I drove home in a state of euphoria, a feeling that in my mind was almost spiritual, close to God-like. It was a feeling that I thought could only come from a deep connection with a man, *this* particular man. In dangerous territory, I felt like a drug addict. The rush was exhilarating.

AFTER THAT FIRST OVERNIGHT SESSION, SETH WAS UN-
predictable. Sometimes we would have our regular hour, and
other times I would be there all night. I lived on the edge each
time I drove to see him. At times, we would simply talk about
life—philosophy, dreams, my problems, his problems—and I
felt honored that he would confide in me. During the times we
would lie on the floor and cuddle, my sexuality would re-
awaken. Seth felt like the umbilical cord to my passion, and I
found it unbearable not to know when I could be with him
next. The intermittent touching, stroking, and cuddling were
not enough. I wanted to move on to the next stage of our relationship.

One day, he said, "Jan, I think you're the kind of woman I
could live with, maybe even marry."

This set my hopes sky-high. I wanted him to make love to
me. *But,* I cautioned myself, *I should wait until the timing is right
since we have the rest of our lives to work on it.*

THE NEXT TIME I SAW SETH, I WAS HOPING TO SPEND THE
night with him. But when I walked into the waiting area, something was different—his appointment calendar wasn't there. He
usually left it sitting out, so I panicked for a moment.

When Seth finally came out, he was dressed in a suit. He
looked like he was going out, but I didn't dare ask. We went
into the therapy room and sat down facing each other. About
forty-five minutes into my session, I heard someone come into
the waiting room. Seth didn't look surprised and wound down
our session, indicating to me that he had another client.

Strange. I was usually his last client of the day.

I had been telling Seth about a problem at work—one of

the men at the office was hinting about asking me out, but I wasn't interested and wanted help in how to handle it. I was also secretly hoping to get a reaction from Seth, that maybe he would be a bit jealous.

Instead, he said our time was up.

"See you next week, Jan," he said matter-of-factly. "I don't have my appointment calendar with me, so I can't check. I may need to change the time. I'll call you to confirm." I rose and he pulled me close for a good-bye hug.

When I walked out, there was a woman I recognized sitting in the waiting room. New to the therapy group, she usually wore casual attire for group sessions, but tonight she was dressed in a short skirt and sexy blouse that revealed her young, firm breasts; she was quite alluring with her curly blond hair and her tall, athletic build. It was obvious she was there for more than a therapy session.

About a month ago, while in group, Seth had mentioned that one of his students was living with him and his girlfriend in his girlfriend's house. Seth had disclosed how proud he was of himself for tutoring her and being a friend to her without it being sexual. He mentioned how they had gone on a long drive together in his motor home, continuing to emphasize the non-sexual nature of their relationship, which at the time, I admit I'd wondered about. He'd since broken up with his girlfriend, but I hadn't realized that all along, the student he'd had living with him was this new member of our group.

Her name was Denise.

As I looked at her and sensed Seth's need to rush me out of the office, it all became clear to me what was going on. My heart sank.

I went home after that therapy session and wondered obsessively about what Seth and Denise were up to. At the group session later that week, I noticed them exchanging long, deep looks, and the chemistry between them was obvious. Our group was supposed to be about honesty and integrity, but neither Seth nor Denise spoke of their obvious sexual connection, and I felt betrayed.

I wanted desperately to believe they were just friends, although I suspected they were lovers. I was unwilling to go there, though, because I didn't want to believe that Seth had anyone else as special as me in his life.

Seth never called to confirm our next appointment, so I finally called him. We agreed I should come in the following Tuesday, our usual day. When he insisted on setting the appointment a little earlier than usual, I stiffened.

TUESDAY DAWNED WINDY AND WARM. I DIDN'T LIKE THE wind—it was too unpredictable, too out of control. I wanted it to stop and be calm again. My mind was working overtime trying to make sense of this Denise thing.

We had never talked about us being in a relationship, but he had definitely led me to believe that we had been developing one. Now, I didn't know what to think, and I felt awkward bringing it up directly, not having the courage to share my true feelings.

The waiting room was empty when I arrived, and I waited for only moments before Seth emerged and we went into his office. Throughout the entire session, I felt there was an elephant in the room we were both ignoring. When we finished, he sat beside me and put what felt like a kindly arm around my shoulders. I looked him in the eye. Sensing that he was about to say something I might resist, I drew in a breath and braced myself.

"Jan, I would like you to consider something." He paused.

I nodded. "What?"

"I think it would help if we included another woman in your next session, to help you with your intimacy issues."

What? Where is this going?

"I think you need to open up more. Bringing this woman in might help you a lot. She's open and honest and spontaneous, and I think it would be good for you."

I knew he was talking about Denise, even though neither of us mentioned her name. I reasoned that at least we'd be in the same room, so I'd have a chance to get to know her better and feel out what was going on between them. I quickly convinced myself that this was all for my healing. I was fast approaching thirty and I wanted to get on with my life, but I still felt a bit uneasy about his proposal.

"I guess that would be okay," I said.

It never occurred to me that he might be doing this for himself, that he would get a kick out of being with two women.

12

BETRAYAL

WHEN THE DAY OF MY SESSION ARRIVED, I ONCE again couldn't decide what to wear. I wanted to be comfortable and wear clothes that were easy to remove, something that wouldn't wrinkle, so I chose some pink leggings and a long, fitted sweater. Unsure if I should wear a bra, I ended up putting on a pretty one I had recently bought.

A part of me couldn't wait to get to Seth's office; another part of me felt a twinge of jealousy at the thought of Denise being there. I felt sick to my stomach imagining him choosing her over me, but this session was supposed to be about my healing and me, and I was determined to learn more about myself, to be open to what this night had to offer me. I didn't know what to expect, but I trusted Seth to take care of me. He had promised this was going to be good for me and I had made the choice to go with it.

I arrived on time and Denise was already there, dressed in a sexy blouse with no bra and jeans that fit her like a glove. Seeing them in Seth's office sipping tea and laughing, I sank into myself and felt smaller than ever.

"You look sexy tonight, Jan," Seth said.

At least he thinks I'm attractive. That's a good start. "Thank you," I said.

The room had a welcoming and romantic ambiance. The lights were dim. Soft music was playing. Candles lit the room.

Denise and Seth looked at each other and then started to take off their clothes. It seemed natural to them, like they had done this before.

I'm not sure I'm ready for this. Aren't we here to talk?

"Jan, Denise and I want to help you. We want you to feel comfortable," Seth said reassuringly.

Then he and Denise got on the floor together, touching each other and beckoning me to join them.

"It's okay, Jan. Take off your clothes and come here."

The shadows from the candles danced on the walls, and the dim light made Denise's muscle tone and smooth skin enticing. I could feel a pull to join them. I didn't want to be left out, so I took a deep breath, trying to calm my nerves, then slowly took off my clothes and joined them on the floor.

Seth and Denise welcomed me with open arms, making room for me in the middle. I slowly lay down between them, feeling both of their bodies warm against mine and smelling the subtle flowery sweetness of Denise's body.

I suddenly felt warm, secure, and desired.

Without thinking, I reached over and began gently stroking Denise's arm. Her body felt so soft and familiar that it could have been my own.

This must be how it feels for a man to touch my body.

I naturally gravitated to other parts of Denise's body, feeling her soft yet firm breasts, her taut stomach, moving down her legs and back up. Denise remained open, lovingly and gently touching me in return.

I looked over at Seth as he lay there watching us. I could tell that he was enjoying what he was seeing unfolding in front of him. Then his firm hands began to massage my head.

I lost track of time as I surrendered to the waves of ecstasy pulsing through me. There was nothing I wanted more than to stay where I was, for this moment to last forever. As night fell and the room became cooler, Seth put a blanket over my shivering body. Denise got up and walked over to the couch, giving Seth a knowing, passionate look. He nodded, returning her gaze.

I tensed up, aware of the sexual energy pulsating between them.

Seth took my hand and whispered in my ear. "Jan, Denise and I want to spend some time alone now."

Was he kidding? I wasn't finished, and I didn't want to leave. I wanted to stay with them all night, wake up together, and then go to breakfast and talk about our experience together. *How can they do this to me?*

As I struggled with why he was rejecting me, I looked over at Denise but she didn't meet my eyes. She was now writing in her journal, waiting for me to leave so she could be alone with Seth.

"So I have to leave now?" I said.

"Yes," Seth said, his voice soft and his tone apologetic. "We'll talk about this another time."

Stunned, I forced myself to get up, put my clothes on, and walk out to my car. Sitting there alone, I imagined them lying in each other's arms, completing what we had all started together.

I drove away in shock, thinking, *Maybe I should go back. How could they kick me out like that? I'm in love with Seth. Don't they know that? How dare they exclude me!*

I drove on automatic pilot. It was late, and there were few other cars on the road. My energy was still back at Seth's office, and the road was a blur. I was dying to know what they were doing, but I already knew. The knot in the pit of my stomach grew tighter with every breath, making my breathing shallow. I walked into my apartment dazed, not wanting to be there. I didn't want to be anywhere. Alone and abandoned, I felt the void of my life swallowing me up. *I should have known this was coming. The one person I turned to for help betrayed me.*

I picked up the phone and called Seth's office number. He answered.

"Seth, I'm feeling so left out," I moaned. "Can't I come back?"

"No, I'm sorry," he said gently. "Denise and I want to spend some time alone."

I hung up the phone and began to cry.

The voice gently called to me from deep within myself, *"I love you, Jan. I'm here."* But I was in too much pain to believe it.

I was falling ... falling into the unknown, just as I had when I was a baby that day with my father, but with no awareness of comforting hands to catch me. The safety net I felt I had built with Seth was gone. Deeper and deeper I fell, my heart breaking into a million pieces.

AFTER THAT NIGHT, I REPEATEDLY TRIED TO RECONNECT with Seth but was unable to reach him. When I called him one last time, desperate to resolve our misunderstanding, he finally picked up.

"I'm feeling so lost and vulnerable," I told him. "It was *my* session. You invited Denise to be with us for one of my sessions, and then you wanted to be alone with her. I don't get it. That night was supposed to be about *my* healing. What happened?"

Silence.

"I need to see you at least one more time," I pleaded, "to help me work through this. Please, Seth."

"I was your therapist, Jan. There will be nothing more between you and me moving forward. Denise and I are in love. Someday you'll find the right person for you too. I'm sorry, Jan. I can't help you anymore."

I heard a click.

He was done with me.

THE NEXT DAY I RECEIVED A CALL FROM BETH, LETTING me know that the group had been discontinued. I tried to get more information from her, but she wouldn't share. When I tried to talk to her about what had happened with Seth—unclear if she already knew—she refused to talk about it in depth with me.

I considered reaching out to others in the group, but it was evident at that point that Seth had abandoned not just me, but also everyone else, for Denise. Most of the people in the group I'd bonded with had already moved on.

My grief was stronger than I could handle, my anger deeper than I could reach. Once again I was left out in the cold, trying to figure out where I had messed up. Day after day I wandered aimlessly through my life, listless and empty, devoid of hope.

A few weeks later, I came home after work and lay down on the floor, giving myself over to the voice of John Denver. His sweet voice was soothing, and the song lyrics guided me to a place inside that was calm and peaceful, where everything made sense and I felt loved and supported. The pain was not gone, but I felt better.

When I questioned who I could trust, I knew it wasn't myself. But although I didn't seem to be making the right decisions about my life, I also knew that there was something beyond all this, something true and clear and free. The problem was, I didn't know how to reach it. I was in too much pain to go within and search for direction; I needed someone else to show me the way. But who? I had trodden the path to betrayal too many times.

The familiar voice inside me called me home through the music.

"Jan, I love you."

Who was this voice?

So many questions, but still no clear answers.

⸎

An Inside Job

NINETEEN SEVENTY-NINE MARKED MY THIRTY-second birthday, and two years since Joel and I divorced.

I was working at a secretarial service in Orange County, grateful to have skills that enabled me to earn enough money to survive. I would drive to Hollywood a couple of times a month to see my family, and I was always welcomed, especially by the younger siblings still at home, who would run out onto the lawn to greet me. It was comforting to be home, but it wouldn't take long for me to tire of the chaos and the memories of childhood. After a day in that environment, I was relieved to return to the quiet of my apartment.

But being alone was digging an even deeper hole inside my heart. I was craving a community of people who were more in tune with who I was, or rather, who I was becoming.

Sometimes I would visit Christine, who was living with her mom. When we didn't have dates on Saturday nights, we would console each other, watching *The Love Boat* and *Fantasy Island* as we dreamed of the lives we truly wanted.

After giving up on God in college, losing my marriage, and being betrayed by an unlicensed therapist I'd thought I could trust, I wasn't sure where I could turn. The Catholic

Church did not feel like a safe refuge to me, and God felt too distant and heartless. I was fine giving up on the whole religion thing.

To fill the void, I began to explore classes at the local community college. I was drawn to a Tai Chi class and signed up. The woman who taught it seemed so at peace with herself. She would do a short meditation with us before and after class, which was comforting to me. I began to feel both re-energized and calm as I practiced the movements over and over again both in class and at home.

One night a different teacher named Anna came in to teach the class. She, too, exuded peace and calm. She was beautiful with long, blonde hair, and she appeared to glow from the inside.

Before practicing our usual Tai Chi moves, Anna led us in a longer meditation. She directed us to focus awareness on the area just above the top of our heads, imagining a white light in the form of a star. She then told us to let that light, or star, open, releasing a downpour of cleansing and purifying light energy, like refreshing spring water. I felt that energy flow over and throughout my entire body, all the way through the soles of my feet, where it dispersed down into the earth beneath me. Anna then directed us to close our feet and let the light fill us and spill out into the space around us. When we felt ready, she said to open our eyes.

After it was over, she asked us how we were doing and if there was anything we wanted to report. Not clear on what I had experienced, I didn't volunteer anything, but I was certain I wanted to do this again and stayed after class to find out more. Anna shared about a practice called Actualism that involved this kind of meditation on a regular basis. When I expressed an interest, she gave me a brochure and invited me to a beginning meditation group that was starting soon.

Drawn to the concept of the light that seemed so freeing, inclusive, and loving, I wondered if it could be the same as God, or perhaps better.

WHEN I ARRIVED AT THE INTRODUCTORY ACTUALISM class that Anna taught, there was no big church or scary priest, no statues to light candles to, and no overly euphoric people. Just a small room with a few chairs: one bigger, cushioned chair for the teacher, and smaller chairs for the few who were beginners like me. There was another woman there about my age and a good-looking blond surfer-type guy. A few others trickled in after us.

Anna's voice was soothing as she guided us through the meditation, similar to the one we had done in class, but with more time to assimilate and report our feelings.

As I listened to her words and tried to follow, I was distracted by all the uninvited thoughts in my head that interfered with the flow of light energy she talked about. I wondered if maybe they were obstructions related to my worry and anxiety.

Then I heard Anna say something that I hadn't heard before.

"Thought directs energy, energy follows thought."

That's interesting, I thought, even though I couldn't quite grasp it.

Then my thoughts began taking over.

How long is this going to take? Maybe I can get Joel to do this and we'll get back together. The guy in this class is really cute. I wonder if he has a girlfriend. He probably likes the other woman here. She's pretty. They'll get together and have a wonderful relationship, leaving me once again in the dust.

I saw them riding off into the sunset together. Laughing, glowing, happy.

As Anna closed the meditation, I experienced a rush of energy through my body, a tingling, a feeling of peace and good will. Anna then answered our questions and concluded the session.

Some of us lingered afterwards and talked outside the office for a while. The woman about my age was named Teri and was easy to talk to. I didn't know it then, but Teri and I would eventually become lifelong friends. We discovered many common interests and quickly developed a deep connection. We also kept each other grounded in the real world as we continued our Actualism practice.

I was hooked, in a good way. The feeling was so soothing that I couldn't stay away—and what was different was that it was coming from inside of me. In the past with Rocko and Seth, I had been hooked because of my lusting attraction for them and the hope that they would fix me. But this was not about sexual desire or being fixed. This was about what was within me, and feelings came up automatically. When I reflected on what Anna had said about thought directing energy and energy following thought, I was curious if my thoughts were indeed controlling my feelings, if I could learn to control them and think only good thoughts.

I knew it wasn't good to deny the bad feelings—that hadn't gotten me anywhere in the past. But as the good feelings came up, so did some bad ones, like anger and fear. We were encouraged to let these feelings surface and then allow them to be consumed in the fires that would transmute them into positive energy.

I was aware that something was happening inside of me, and I wanted it to continue. I was tired of feeling lost and alone, and I wanted to heal everything that had been in the way of being my true self in the world.

Actualism was a step-by-step process that I practiced

regularly, no matter what was going on in my life. Some people thought it was strange, but I didn't care. I attended the classes and did a meditation session, even if just a short one, almost daily.

But as I was beginning to get the sense that the answer was inside of me, my brain still longed for a quick fix. I wanted to be free *now*, and Actualism didn't work that way. While the road ahead of me was uncertain, however, I still had the comforting voice coming from inside. I didn't know what it meant, or whose voice it was, but I knew one thing for sure: that voice had never left me.

14

⸙

BACK HOME

*I*N 1982, I DECIDED TO MOVE BACK IN WITH MY PARENTS for a while and continue my education. So I left Orange County and returned to Hollywood, the place where it all began.

I felt like something had gone wrong and I needed to fix it, to start over, to find the life I was supposed to be living—a normal life where I could fall in love, get married, have children, and have a fulfilling career.

I was determined to find answers, and it was pretty clear to me at this point that it had everything to do with what was going on inside of me, my perspective, and what I was attracting. By the time I was thirty-five, I had been going to Actualism classes faithfully for a few years, and even though classes were also accessible near my parents' home, I felt I needed a break from it. I was curious what I would do with this new version of me in an old environment.

I enrolled at a university in Los Angeles for the purpose of completing my Bachelor's degree, and I found a job at a company in the San Fernando Valley that sold video equipment. Rick was the manager of this previously successful small company that was now experiencing a downturn—he had been hired to save the day, and I understood why. Not only did people seem to respect him, but he appeared to be on top of everything, speaking clearly and with a sense of authority. He was a sizeable man of about forty, with dark, slicked-back hair, big ears like Clark Gable, and a commanding presence that I found attractive.

Someone had mentioned that he was married.

Jan, I told myself, *go no further.*

I was making copies one day when Rick came around behind me.

"Sexy dress," he whispered as he brushed past me.

I felt that familiar tingle run through my body.

Rick then began to pay more attention to me, finding excuses to come by my desk and make a comment or tell me a joke. His voice resonated with sexual overtones.

"Can I bring you some coffee?" Rick offered one afternoon.

"Yes, that would be nice."

He came back five minutes later with a fresh cup of coffee and a donut.

"Anything else I can do for you?"

I wanted to say something witty, but my knees got weak and the blood rushed to my face, so I ended up saying nothing.

Because of Rick, work suddenly became exciting, and I began to look forward to seeing him. I couldn't help myself. I was once again hooked into that inexplicable energy that connects two people. It was like a drug, and I could never seem to get enough.

Hearing Rick was married was one thing, but seeing his wife was another. One day, she showed up at the office while I was at the front desk. Not knowing who she was, I asked her if I could help her. She was a beautiful, fiery woman with red hair who seemed the perfect combination of matronly and sexy. Instead of answering me, though, she walked straight into Rick's office. It was impossible not to hear the yelling back and forth, and it sounded like someone was pounding on the desk. She stormed out of the office a few minutes later, and I heard tires screeching as she tore out of the parking lot.

Rick emerged from his office and merely shrugged his shoulders, his look conveying that he felt disgusted and helpless. I didn't ask what had happened, but we never saw his wife again. I heard rumors that she had left him for good.

Wake up, Jan.

I heard that all too familiar inner voice in the distance but didn't pay much attention to it.

ONE NIGHT, RICK STOPPED BY MY DESK ON HIS WAY OUT for the day, and asked me out for that Friday night.

Here was my chance. I couldn't think of any reason to say no. "Sure," I said, doing my best to sound nonchalant.

Friday night couldn't come soon enough for me. My body was tingling with desire. When it finally arrived, we left together after work, being careful to avoid running into anyone from the office. He escorted me to his car and opened my door first to let me in and make sure I was comfortable. I had taken the bus to work that day, expecting to be driven home after our date.

As he held his warm hand over mine while he drove, I could hardly bear the waves of energy coursing through my body. When he stopped at a red light, leaned over, and kissed me, I didn't object.

Oh my God!

After taking me to dinner at an old-fashioned steak house, Rick took me to the low-class motel he was staying in since his wife left him. He didn't even have a home of his own, but I didn't care. It was in that sleazy motel that I experienced some of the best orgasms ever, over and over again. Somehow, despite his volatility and lack of stability, Rick knew how to please a woman, at least in the moment. But once again, I was being led by my hormones and ignoring my voice of reason.

WE HAD BEEN DATING FOR A FEW WEEKS WHEN RICK came over to meet my parents. I was in the passenger seat as he pulled his car that I called a boat straight up the steep driveway and up onto the lawn as if he were too good for the cement. Then, chest out, hair slicked back, wearing a white T-shirt with rolled-up sleeves for his cigarettes, he got out and walked toward the house ahead of me.

I thought he was sexy, and I expected my parents to like him.

When Mom came out to greet us after seeing us pull up, she smiled and invited us in, but I sensed her immediate disapproval. After that, I was hyper-aware of everyone's response and strove to control how they were acting, as I had so hopelessly tried to do when I was a child.

While we were there, Rick leaned over and whispered in my ear, "I want you to have my baby."

Too much too soon. I definitely was not ready for a baby, and I didn't know Rick well enough to consider the idea with him. But despite knowing it wasn't the right time, I melted when he said those words. With the pleasant tickle of his breath in my ear, fantasies of the perfect family flooded my senses.

Once again, I ignored all the obvious red flags.

A FEW NIGHTS LATER, RICK CALLED FROM A BAR WITH the telltale slur in his speech I knew so well from Joel.

"I want you, Jan," he said. "Please come over here and get me."

"Rick, it's late."

"You fucking whore," he yelled. "Get your butt over here, if you know what's good for you."

I stopped breathing. I figured he didn't realize what he had said, or maybe he was just being funny.

Then I heard the sound of the dial tone.

Against my better judgment, I let our relationship progress, and one night Rick asked if he could invite my parents out to dinner so he could ask them for my hand in marriage.

How considerate, how respectful, how charming and old-fashioned.

The fact that he was not yet divorced was far from my mind.

Over dinner at a nice restaurant in Hollywood that was intended to impress my parents, Rick took advantage of a lull in the conversation to say, "I love your daughter very much, and I want to marry her."

Dad responded by grinning from ear to ear—seemingly happy that I had found someone who wanted to take care of me—but the look on Mom's face was not so obliging. It was more like, "Okay, prove it."

After that night, Rick asked me to move in with him, promising he'd find us a place to live, but I wasn't sure I was ready to leave the security of my parents' house.

"You can't stay with them forever," Rick taunted. "It's time to move on. We'll make a life together."

"Okay," I conceded. But despite being unsure that this was the right move, I was afraid of losing him if I didn't do what he wanted.

"I'm in the fast lane and I want you to come with me," he said.

When I told my family I was moving in with him, Mom asked, "Are you sure this is what you want?"

"Yes," I assured her, "it's time for me to move on, and he wants us to live together. I'm in love with him."

My mother held her tongue, knowing there was no changing my mind.

Christine was another story.

Gathering my nerve, I called to tell her that I was moving in with Rick. We had gone out to dinner with Christine and her husband recently, and it seemed to go well, or so I thought.

She gave only a perfunctory "Oh" in response to my news until I pushed her, and even then she was reluctant to say more, a sure sign that she had a strong opinion she was not ready to share.

"We're just concerned about you," was all she could muster.

I was not entirely surprised that she didn't approve, but I was hoping she would at least pretend to be happy for me. Even though I always wanted the truth from Christine, it was sometimes difficult to swallow. Her opinion mattered a lot to me, nonetheless.

There was an uncomfortable silence on the other end of the phone.

"Christine, don't you have anything else to say?"

"No. Not really."

"Well, what do you think?"

"I think it's a bad idea."

There it was. Clearly she didn't understand what Rick and I had, and truthfully, I didn't want to know what she was thinking.

THE HOME RICK FOUND FOR US WAS AN UNFINISHED two-story guesthouse in someone's backyard. The man who was building it promised to finish it within a few weeks, so we moved in. With no furniture beyond a futon to sleep on, it wasn't exactly my dream home, but I reassured myself that it was only temporary.

Aside from the lack of furniture, living with Rick presented other challenges. I quickly realized that he didn't want me to spend time with anyone but him. He seemed resentful of my family, my friends, anything that didn't involve him. He would become irrationally upset when I received phone calls from anyone. What's more, he acted threatened by the fact that I was attending school and discouraged me from continuing, even after I explained to him that it was important to me to finally finish my Bachelor's degree, and that I was disappointed he wasn't supporting me in my dreams.

The only place he wanted to take me out was to a local bar where people knew him. It was disheartening to watch him pick fights easily and drink too much, but when I asked myself what I was doing with a man like that, I had no answer except the magnetic attraction I could not seem to ignore.

After the company found out that Rick and I were dating, they let me go, so I had to find a part-time job to keep up with my share of the expenses. Soon after—due to poor work performance and losing his temper one too many times—Rick got fired too. After that, it fell on me to pay the rent. Not only that, but his job loss meant that he lost the car, since "the boat" belonged to the company. Scared of how he'd take the loss, I bought him a used car that looked big and boat-like. It only cost about $200 and needed some work, but I hoped it would play into his need to feel big and powerful, at least on the road.

As fearful as I was of him, I was still irrationally dedicated to making the relationship work.

ONE NIGHT I CAME HOME LATE FROM A CLASS. I KNEW there might be consequences for getting home later than usual, but I was feeling rebellious and angry about giving up my freedom. I had noticed that Rick was starting to drink heavily during the day, and he was monitoring me closely, watching my every move. As I'd been driving, I realized that I didn't want to go home at all—Rick and I didn't have much of a life, and the place we called home remained unfinished. Plus, I could never predict what kind of mood he would be in.

How dare he control my life like this? I thought. It didn't dawn on me that I was allowing it.

When I pulled into the driveway, the downstairs was dark but I noticed a light on upstairs. As I headed up, I heard the phone slam down.

"Where have you been?" Rick yelled. "I've called everyone I know trying to find you. I even called the police!"

"I stayed late to study with some friends," I said, trying not to upset him more.

"Stop lying!" He shouted. "I know you were out with a man. You're always sneaking around to meet men. At school. At the gym. You're a slut. Admit it."

Terrified I would say the wrong thing and escalate him further, I said, "Rick, that's not true. You know you're the only man in my life. I don't want to be with anyone else."

"Don't lie to me."

Paralyzed with fear, I didn't know what to say or do.

Then, without warning, he grabbed me by my shirt collar and shoved me up against the wall. When I looked into his eyes, I saw a monster, a raging beast with intense, scary eyes.

He slapped me first with one hand and then with the other, then he pulled my sweater off.

I was too scared to fight back, so I merely cringed, hoping he wouldn't knock my teeth out. Not wanting to scream and disturb anyone, I imagined it was only a nightmare. But it didn't end.

"You dirty slut!" Rick yelled in my face. "You women are all sluts!"

I thought for sure I was going to die as I questioned *Who is this man? What am I doing here?*

I wanted to run, to get as far away from him as possible, but I couldn't move. The wall behind me was my only support. He kept yelling at me, pulling at my clothes, holding me against the wall, and slapping me repeatedly. I tried as best I could to protect my face and keep my clothes on, but I was getting weaker by the minute.

At last he let go, and I fell to the floor. Pain coursed through my lip, and my clothing was torn. Childhood scenes flashed through my head, scenes from the days when I always had to second guess Dad, to sidestep him and become invisible.

Rick was Dad, only Dad wasn't here.

I thought I had gotten away from my father, but obviously I hadn't. My body was telling me that this was the same, that I was trapped. Waves of guilt and shame swept over me as I heard the familiar voices in my head.

You're not doing it right. It's your fault.

I wanted to hide, but there was nowhere to hide, just like at home. I froze, feeling nothing in my body. I couldn't move, and I was consumed by voices in my head.

Maybe I deserved this. Maybe I'm being punished for doing something wrong. I should have gotten home on time. I should be a better partner. I shouldn't be so selfish. Maybe I should give up school, even if I don't want to.

I could barely move, though I wanted to run. If I could have, I would have gotten up, dashed to my car, and driven away. But where would I go? Not to my parents' house. He might come after me and hurt my family. Not to Christine.

We hadn't spoken since that day she told me it was a bad idea to move in with Rick. Not to my brothers. They'd probably kill him. No one would understand.

I looked over then and saw Rick curled up on the floor in a fetal position.

"I'm so sorry," he sobbed. "I didn't mean it. Please forgive me."

As I sat there frozen, realizing I had nowhere to go, he crawled over and lay in a huddle at my feet, begging me to forgive him.

Shocked and feeling sorry for him, I held his head on my lap as he cried like a baby.

"Let's go to bed, sweetie," he sobbed. "I promise this will never happen again."

But I knew then that it wasn't going to get better.

I WOKE UP THE NEXT MORNING AND LOOKED OVER TO see Rick sleeping peacefully. I crawled out of bed, then raised my aching body up and looked into the mirror. My lip was swollen, and my eyes were red and puffy from crying, but I got myself quietly ready for school and left anyway.

If anyone asks, I reasoned, *I can say I stayed up late to study and that I bit my lip.*

But glancing in the rearview mirror and seeing how pathetic I looked, I decided not to go to class after all. Instead, I went to my parents' house.

"Are you okay, Jan?" Mom asked, happy to see me but clearly concerned.

I did my best not to cry, but tears ran down my face. "I'm okay, Mom. I just had a bad night. I got home from school kind of late last night."

"What happened to your lip?"

"Oh. I think I bit it."

I could tell she didn't believe me. I was not used to lying, and I wasn't good at it.

"Are things okay with you and Rick?" she asked.

"Yeah. He just misses me when I'm gone too much."

"That's how men are," she said, trying to reassure me.

That's what she honestly believes, I thought. I had heard it many times as a child. Afraid to stand up to Dad, she let us get abused. When the incident ended, she simply moved on, keeping her marriage intact.

Doesn't she understand what that did to us?

On some level, though, I realized that she must have felt powerless in her life. Mom had certainly wanted the abuse to stop, but she probably felt like she couldn't do anything to make that happen. She was afraid, and where could she have run with all us kids?

Then I remembered what she had once told me, that when she got married she decided to let her husband be the boss. She didn't want to be like her mother, who was the strong one. It was the man's job to be the strong one, she said, and so she let Dad have the power.

Unwittingly, perhaps shockingly, I attracted the same thing into my life.

As I rehearsed in my mind how I would tell Rick that I was leaving, an unnerving dialogue was taking place.

"Rick, this isn't working for me. I'm not happy. I'm going to move back in with my parents."

Don't tell him where you're going, the inner voice cautioned. *He'll come after you. He'll hurt you, and he'll hurt your family.*

"Rick, I need to take a break for a while."

He'll think you're coming back.

"Rick, this isn't working for me. I'm going to find someplace else to live."

"Rick, I'm not happy. I need some time by myself."

Okay. Close enough.

But when I finally found the courage to tell him I wanted to leave, he convinced me to stay.

"Please don't leave," he implored. "We can work this out. I just need more time to get this new deal going. Jan, I'll change. I'll make it up to you."

I gave in.

But nothing changed, and I continued to live in fear.

ON THANKSGIVING, WE DROVE TO MY FAMILY'S HOUSE for the usual feast. I wanted the day to be normal; as far as my family knew, Rick was still the man I was planning to marry, but I was uncomfortable the whole time. The more he drank, the more unsettled I felt, and I caught him giving my sisters inappropriate looks.

"You look sexy today," he said to my younger sister Sue.

She did look sexy. She always did—and she always got the guys. But why did his flirtation bother me so much? Did I really want him after what he'd done to me? Why was I questioning whether he liked me better than Sue? Was this what I deserved?

After dinner, my brothers headed downstairs, and I suspected they would probably do drugs—pot, cocaine, they were always in supply. So when Rick followed them, I cringed.

When the guys came back upstairs, Rick was slurring his words and acting arrogant and hostile. And then I heard him arguing with my brother Mark.

"You don't know what the hell you're talking about!" Rick shouted.

Mocking him, Mark gave my brother Paul a knowing glance and rolled his eyes.

At that moment Rick made another remark to Sue. "Are you related to these jerks? They don't deserve such a classy sister."

Sue smiled coyly, appreciating the attention.

At that point, I managed to convince Rick it was time for us to leave. As Mom walked us to the door, I gave her a look, hoping she would somehow save me, but she didn't.

I searched her eyes, confused. *Doesn't she get that I'm not safe?*

But it wasn't her job to save me, it was mine.

AS TIME PASSED AND I STAYED WITH RICK, I MADE SCHOOL my greatest focus. Despite not having the courage to leave him, I was determined to move forward. I had a new part-time job, and I was going to the gym regularly. Not wanting to give any of that up, I tried to maintain some semblance of normalcy. I was terrified of change and avoided intimacy with others for fear they would discover my secret and force me to see my situation more clearly.

Isolated and alone, I worried every day that I might say or do something that would call out Rick's monster. At the end of the day I would come home and sit down with him and watch TV shows—reruns from an earlier time where people laughed and everything turned out okay in the end. He seemed to like this routine, and it kept us from dealing with the reality of our situation. I knew I couldn't stay, but I was terrified of making a move.

Finally, after about a month of living in constant fear of being hit again, I could no longer put off the decision to leave.

I came out of the bathroom one morning and sat down on the bed as Rick was waking up. I said with conviction, "Rick, I'm leaving."

All he said was, "Well, maybe I'll go back to Ohio for a while and stay with my mom."

Huh? I had expected him to resist, and when he didn't, I was scared that he might change his mind, or that his mood might switch dramatically again. If I was going to get out, it had to be now.

After calling Mom and telling her I was coming back home, I packed up my belongings that day and drove to my parents' house. Dad was standing on the front lawn when I drove up.

Embarrassed and ashamed, I was on the verge of tears; my father was the last person I wanted to see. I got out of my car, eyes lowered, hoping to make it into the house without having to look up. But instead, Dad walked directly to me. He put his arms out and hugged me, silently, without any questions. For the first time, it was as though he understood how much pain I was in.

ABOUT A MONTH LATER, THE PHONE RANG IN THE MIDDLE of the night. It was the police. They wanted to know if I was missing a credit card, saying they had arrested a man for car theft in Indiana who had a credit card of mine in his possession. The man turned out to be Rick. "Do you know him?" they asked. I said yes, that I used to, but wanted nothing more to do with him.

After I talked to the police, I lay in my bed and heard the distant voice, louder than usual.

Jan, it's time to reclaim your power. You deserve to be loved and cherished, not disrespected and slapped around. Wake up!

I'd been emotionally shut down for so long that I hadn't realized how much anger I had stuffed deep inside of me, and under that anger was grief—grief for the woman I'd let die. I understood then that I'd been in denial about why I had attracted such a monster. Was I afraid of the monster inside of myself, the one that could be unleashed at any moment and hurt someone, like Dad did? I was finally beginning to realize that I couldn't change anything outside of myself until I dealt with what was inside of me.

Maybe it was time to get back to Actualism, and possibly therapy. But could I trust another therapist?

15

WHAT IS THIS GOD THING?

$\mathcal{I}$T WAS 1994. MY FRIEND TERI—WHO I HAD MET through Actualism—and I were in our forties now and had known each other for quite some time. Both of us were working in downtown Los Angeles, and we would meet for lunch about once a week.

But on this particular day, as we sat down to eat, I noticed something different about her. She was wearing colorful scarves that accentuated her graceful and flowing demeanor, and she was glowing from the inside—the love pouring out of her was palpable.

We had missed lunch the previous two weeks because Teri said she was taking time off work to go to some kind of Intensive or workshop that a friend of hers had done, and her life was never the same. She didn't know much about it herself, but she was going.

We had often shared our mutual frustrations with our lives—I was dissatisfied with working downtown and catering to the needs of rich attorneys, and though I was grateful to have a job as a legal secretary in a prestigious law firm, which had given me more financial stability than ever in my life, I wanted more. Teri, too, had her complaints about work. But today she expressed wanting to quit her job and move into a spiritual community in a peaceful area away from the city.

"Wow," I said. "Is it because of that Intensive you told me about?"

Teri flashed me a big smile and nodded. "Jan, all I can say is that I am more open than I've ever been in my entire life. I am so happy to be here in this moment, with you."

She reached over and took my hand, looking me in the eyes as if she were looking through me to my soul.

"Every single moment of my life is exciting now," she said. "My whole perspective has changed. I'm in love with God, with myself, with everyone."

When the waitress walked up to take our order, Teri pulled her hand away and said with enthusiasm, "I'll have a hamburger with everything on it."

"What?" I said. "You never eat meat. What's up?"

She merely smiled as I gave my order. After the waitress left, I gave Teri a palms-up shrug, urging her to explain.

"Well," she began, "one thing I've learned through this experience is that I can make decisions in the moment and not worry. I want meat, so I'm letting myself have it. It's amazing what happens when your heart breaks open."

I'd had my heart broken many times, and it never felt good to me. I remembered how destroyed I'd felt when Joel asked me for a divorce.

My eyes widened. "Your heart breaking open is a good thing?"

"Yes, Jan. It's so amazing. My heart opened like it's never opened before. It's not like a breakup. It's a lightness, a love. The Intensive is a place where I really felt okay to open up and feel it all. When I allowed it to happen, I was more than okay. I could actually feel the love moving through me. I reached a point in the Intensive where I was no longer in denial, or holding back. I was open, and so was everyone else. It was such a safe and loving environment, the kind of atmosphere we should have grown up in, but didn't, because our parents didn't know any better."

I reflected on how Mom believed the past was the past and there was no need to rehash it. She said that when she married Dad, she decided to let the past go and live her new life. But that wasn't working for me. Then, when I had tried opening myself up in a group, and with Seth in one-on-one sessions, I was shut down again by betrayal. Yes, I had experienced openings in my heart in Actualism in subtle ways, but what Teri was talking about seemed different, more explosive and exciting.

Her energy was intoxicating, but was it just a temporary fix? And what was all this God talk? She was speaking about God so openly and freely, as if He or She were real, and right there with us.

I was a little uncomfortable with the concept of God. Growing up in Catholic school, I was afraid of making mistakes and committing sins for fear I would go to hell, or at least purgatory, potentially for eternity. Now, Teri was introducing me to something that felt real. Could the Intensive be my opportunity to explore what God was for me? Could God be as real and tangible as Teri was suggesting? I thought about the movie *Oh, God!*, in which God was portrayed as real and approachable, like a wise friend.

Teri handed me a brochure that said "Angels of God" on the front.

"Here's some info about it, Jan. Check it out."

After lunch, we went our separate ways, but she caught up to me before I drove away and placed a cassette tape in my hand.

"They gave me this at the Intensive," she said. "Listen to

it. Or don't. But please treat it with care. I probably shouldn't give this to you. It's pretty potent. But I think you can handle it."

That night, on the way home from work, I slipped the tape in my cassette player and began to listen.

A woman's voice introduced a man who had such a strong desire for God that it had brought God's energy into his body and transformed him into a fully enlightened being. She said he was an incarnation of God.

I had been fooled many times, so I was skeptical. But when his voice came on, something stirred inside of me. I felt as though he were talking directly to me.

Traffic had slowed to a crawl, which in Los Angeles was normal, but it usually frustrated me beyond words, sometimes resulting in a scream to release the tension. At that moment, however, listening to that tape while ensconced in my car and trapped in gridlock, I felt completely content.

"God is real," he was saying. "He's right here with you in your life. But to experience God, you have to let go of the illusion of separation. The truth is, God is a loving and accepting being who wants you to be happy. The illusion is not real, but it will do its best to convince you that it is. You have been taught the illusion of separation, proving that God is above you and you could never be worthy enough, as you continue to die and take birth again, with the same message over and over again."

I thought of the Catholic Church and how brainwashed I had been, believing that I was never good enough or perfect enough—which was also reinforced by Dad.

"I can show you how to break the cycle of birth and death and come home to your True Self."

What is he talking about? What home?

Something began pulling at me from deep down inside. I

knew that when he alluded to breaking the cycle of birth and death, he wasn't talking about physical death. He was talking about surrendering to the person I truly was inside. The illusion part was a revelation too.

I wondered how much of my life was illusion and how much was real, if the abuse I experienced as a child was an illusion, if my parents' love for me was an illusion.

"Desire is everything," he said.

Desire. Is he talking about sex? That desire has gotten me in plenty of trouble. I have desired to have a different life, more money, a different family, but I still feel stuck in my life. Maybe I've desired the wrong things? Could there be a higher desire that would take me through this illusion so I can see what's really here?

"Give up. Let go. Surrender. Let yourself have the love you deserve. You are precious, and God wants you to be happy. Man has tried many ways of getting closer to God. Each person's path is unique. No matter what you do in your search for God, it will never be lost, not even if you are pulled in a different direction from the organization, religion, or spiritual master you are following. You can free yourself to be fully connected with God. All you have to do is keep going. And never give up."

Could this actually be God? How would I recognize if God were calling me?

In high school, I remember reading about saints who had conversations with God like an intimate friend and wondered how they did that. And how did they know it was God? Was it like the quiet voices that have been there all my life? Were they now speaking through this tape, directly to me?

I couldn't get enough of this man's soothing voice, drawing me in, comforting me, melting me, validating my hunger for the truth. It occurred to me that perhaps God and the truth were one and the same. Truth was something I had always valued, even when it hit me in the face and turned my life upside down.

He continued, "It's like a bank account that you keep depositing into. It's there, and it keeps growing, and eventually it will be enough to set you free."

If he was right, it meant that everything I had done before counted. All my efforts to be a good person, to find myself, to actualize my true self, had all been worthwhile.

And I liked that word: free.

I longed to break out of the prison I had created within myself. What if I could bust out of my shell like a newly hatched chick, ready to grow and expand, alive and healthy, filled with unlimited energy and a zest for life? The bank account analogy assured me that I had some control. My personal path, unique to me, was guiding me where I needed to be.

The tape ended before I reached home, so I rewound it and listened again, hanging on to every word. I felt as though I was with a lover I didn't want to leave.

I quickly felt a deep-inside commitment to follow this God energy. I wanted to live in the present, free of concerns about the past and the future. I knew there had to be another side to the anxiety, depression, and hopelessness I had been living with. What I didn't realize at the time was that it was the feelings repressed deep inside of me that would save me.

THE NEXT DAY I CALLED THE NUMBER ON THE BROCHURE for the Angels of God Intensive. The woman who answered the phone, Myra, sounded grounded and real, and she was willing to answer my questions. Not at all pushy or obnoxious, she didn't give me the feeling that she was trying to sell anything.

"Jan, come and meet some of the people who have done the Intensive," she suggested. "We have an intro coming up

Tuesday night. Why don't you stop by? We would love to see you there."

I decided to go. I wanted proof.

THAT TUESDAY NIGHT, NOT KNOWING WHAT TO EXPECT, I walked into a house filled with people for the intro. I did my best to socialize, even though I felt insecure and uptight.

Myra opened the meeting with a general description of the organization's purpose, which she said was to help people break free of "The Illusion" so they could be their true selves. She made it sound possible, like the most normal thing in the world.

After the mingling began, I immediately felt comfortable with the people in the room. They seemed nice, and like me, most of them were nine-to-fivers who had come here straight from the office. Surprisingly, the majority had already done the Intensive; I was one of the few new guests. I wondered if they were collectively trying to talk me into it, having already done the Intensive, but I decided to go with the flow and see what happened.

After a short while, Myra asked others in the room to share about their experiences in the Intensive and how their lives were being affected by it.

One man eagerly stood up and spoke.

"Before I did this Intensive, I was afraid of people," he said. "I was stuck. I couldn't seem to move forward. My life is changing now because I'm open. I broke up with the woman I was dating because I realized she wasn't right for me and that I deserve to be happy. I've met someone else now, and I'm excited about exploring this new relationship. It's real, not based on my illusions of what a relationship is supposed to be like. It's the best one I've ever had."

I couldn't help but question if this big, powerful-looking man had actually been scared of people. What was it about this workshop that made it so easy for him to find the right woman?

Could it work for me to find the right man?

A woman who appeared to be about my age spoke up next.

"I'm experiencing a relationship with God that I never would have thought possible. The religion I was raised in portrayed God as a distant figure out in space, judging me and expecting me to be perfect. At this Intensive I experienced a loving and accepting God, who loves with the unconditional love I've always wanted to give my children but couldn't because I hadn't received it myself. I realized that I don't have to be perfect to be with God," she said.

It was as if she were speaking from inside of me. Striving for perfection to obtain God's approval had caused me a lot of pain in my life. Teri had said the same thing. Suddenly, it was like a bolt of light illuminated my mind.

How would it be if I had been raised with unconditional love? Dad had made me think I had to be perfect, but that was impossible, and I was weary from trying. Maybe I deserved to be happy. And maybe I didn't need to be perfect to be loved.

Just then, a young man glowing with vibrant energy spoke up.

"God is real to me now," he said. "I can feel him. I can touch him. He's all around me. He is in me, and everyone in this room."

I hadn't experienced so much joy in one place before. These people had clearly connected to a place inside filled with unconditional love, a love that according to them was inclusive and not limiting, a love so big it overflowed into the room and embraced us all, without exception. They talked about their relationships with God as if He were their best friend, a lover even.

I wanted what they had and was determined to find a way to do the Intensive.

Despite sensing an easy camaraderie earlier, however, I felt myself tense up as the meeting came to a close, feeling self-conscious and anxious about socializing. But then, I gravitated toward a group of men, one of whom was extremely handsome. As he made lots of eye contact and smiled, I fantasized about him asking me out, finding myself slipping into that same old pattern—insecure but flattered that he was paying attention to me.

I acted coy and chit-chatted a bit, making some disparaging remarks about the past relationships I'd had with men, and then I walked away, not thinking much of our conversation. But a few moments later he showed up, planting himself directly in front of me. He pointed at my heart, and when he spoke, his words pierced me like a sword.

"You need this Intensive," he said. "Your attitude pushes men away. You castrate men with your anger. I have to wonder, what happened to you? Don't you want to be free of that?"

That hit hard. Tears suddenly sprung to my eyes as I thought, *What is he talking about? It's men who have abused ME. Is he saying I punish men because of how I've been hurt?*

I thought about my anger toward my father, toward Joel and Seth and Rick, and I realized I was still angry. Yes, my anger could be keeping men away—and probably women, as well. I thought of my sisters and Evelyn and other strong women in my life whose volatility scared me and kept me from being myself. And Mom? She always seemed to be the peacemaker, but I was becoming more and more aware of her manipulations in her effort to keep the peace. She would urge me to do things I wasn't comfortable doing, like talk to one of my sisters when I didn't want to or get in the middle of what was none of my business. I was like her in ways that caused me to suppress my real feelings and try to be the "good one." I didn't want that job anymore. "Castrate" was a strong word, but somehow I didn't take offense.

The next day, I called Myra and signed up for the Angels of God Intensive.

16

THE INTENSIVE

HERE WASN'T MUCH GOING ON IN MY LIFE WHEN I left for the Intensive. I had an unfulfilling job at the law firm with plenty of unused vacation time, and I happened to be dating a man who was not interested in being in a relationship. I couldn't think of a better way to spend a week or so off—to focus on myself and what was keeping me from feeling happy and fulfilled.

Optimistic that I would finally learn why I kept experiencing frustrating and painful situations in my life over and over again, I felt free as I jumped into my car with my packed bags that Friday afternoon.

I arrived at the hotel in San Diego early enough to check into my room, planning to have dinner by myself. I didn't mind eating alone; I wasn't ready to socialize yet. When I mentioned Angels of God at the front desk, I was given my room number and told I had two roommates: a woman named Sheila and a man named Jim. I was a little puzzled why they would put a man in our room, but I was open to the process.

After dinner, I returned to my hotel room to find that neither Sheila nor Jim had arrived yet. Not wanting to be selfish or cause any trouble, I chose the small foldout bed and left the two queens for them. As I was putting my clothes away, making sure I didn't use too much space, Sheila arrived. She was about my age, and the first thing she said was, "Why did you take the small bed? Let's take the big ones. We got here first."

"You're right!" I said assertively. *Why do I keep deferring to others? This is my time to claim the space I keep being told I deserve.* I moved my stuff to one of the queen beds and immediately felt more open and confident.

Sheila was a perfect roommate match for me. Full of spunk, she was easy to be with and made me laugh, and we connected easily.

In the morning, Sheila and I drove together to the center where the Intensive was being held. The outside of the building looked like an ordinary business center, with parking in the middle and various small offices. Being a Saturday, it was fairly quiet.

Most of the people arriving were headed for the same place we were, and we saw a group heading toward one of the offices. When we walked in, we were greeted by two people with a banner reading "Angels of God" behind them. They received us warmly and directed us to nearby tables with the initial of our first name over it. Sheila and I agreed to reconvene as soon as we had checked in at our respective tables.

As I waited in line, I looked around and saw that the space was big and open, belying the outside appearance of a conservative small business. There were double doors separating the entry room from what I assumed was the main room. People were milling about, some in small groups and some wandering around by themselves. All of them had looks of uncertainty on their faces, as though they didn't know what they were getting into, but they seemed excited to pay their money, get their nametags, and dive in nonetheless.

I filled out the necessary forms and confirmed my payment in full. A woman—who I assumed was already completely "free"—then handed me a liability form to sign, which showed me how serious this was. The form mentioned the possibility of death, for which I would be completely liable.

Oh please, Jan, it's just a form, I told myself.

Then she handed me a nametag. I would no longer be anonymous in this room full of strangers.

My body had begun trembling, but I couldn't tell whether it was from fear or excitement. I knew I'd asked for a challenge, and I was convinced this was going to prove to be a big one.

As I looked around again, trying to find Sheila, I noticed that we were an eclectic mix: young and old, men and women of a range of shapes and sizes. Then I heard strains of music, muffled screams, and what sounded like tapping on a microphone make their way through the adjacent wall.

I found Sheila and stayed close to her.

"What do you think is going on in there?" I asked.

She raised her brow and shrugged. Caught up in the intensity of the moment, we decided to briefly swap background stories.

I told her about the latest man I was currently obsessed with, who seemed to enjoy my company but was not interested in a relationship, and who apparently was impotent. Not even worth mentioning, and yet I couldn't seem to let go. Sheila was fed up with getting hurt by men and determined to get to the bottom of why she kept attracting the wrong kind of men.

"I know," I said, exasperated. "I don't get it. I keep doing the same thing too."

Sheila told me how she was trying to break away from a man she had been living with for several years, but she just couldn't seem to make the split.

"Just leave him!" I said, as if I knew better. "Why would you stay with someone who treats you so badly?"

She looked at me and laughed. "What about you? You don't sound like you've been too successful with men either."

There was an uncomfortable silence, and I could feel my defenses building up.

"We all look like a bunch of hippies waiting for the drug to kick in," Sheila finally said.

I laughed, relieved.

Meanwhile, Jim, our other roommate, found us and introduced himself. He was a younger man, very polite, and tall. Upon seeing his height, I felt bad that he'd been left the foldout bed and apologized to him as if I had done something wrong.

"No worries," he said sincerely. "I grew up with sisters and I'm used to getting the short end of the stick." Then he gave me a big hug. At that moment, I began to realize how unimportant these small details were in the larger picture.

Just then, a guy across the room made eye contact and smiled at me. He had short, curly brown hair and a mischievous, intriguing sort of smile. I noticed that I wasn't the only one he was flirting with, but the looks he sent me made me feel special, like maybe he would choose me.

No, Jan. He's cute, but way too young.

Then he winked.

Oh no, I thought, *I can't do this. I just paid a lot of money to get beyond this kind of danger in my life.*

Knowing this event was supposed to be about me, and that I needed to stay focused and not let myself get distracted, didn't help. I watched him for any sign of attachment; there were people around him, but maybe they were just friends. And even if he was attached to someone, maybe he would change during this Intensive and want to date me.

Stop! I screamed in my head. *Stay focused.*

As I continued observing people, the waiting became uncomfortable. I reminded myself that I didn't actually know any of these people, so I could always hide or pretend I was someone else if I had to. But I wasn't someone else, and my mind was putting me through hell.

Get out while you can, something told me. But I had come too far for that.

I had to admit, the people who were there to guide us through the process struck me as mysterious. Their demeanor was strictly business: efficient and professional. The women were noticeably beautiful with little or no makeup and simple hairstyles, and the men wore black pants and dress shirts with dark ties. They all looked peaceful, yet stern. Despite their mysterious air, I felt they were trustworthy and was glad they had ensured we signed all the necessary papers, not to mention that we were in good shape physically. It was as if they were taking care of all our needs so that we could fully commit to the process.

We had been told to bring towels and a bottle of water; those who didn't remember were sent to another room where they were given what they needed. I found myself immediately judging them for forgetting what they were supposed to bring. *Stop, Jan.*

After over two hours of waiting for everyone to be registered and accounted for, a man came through the double doors. In a stern manner, he instructed us to pick up our towels and water bottles and to form a large circle around the room. The air bristled with a sense of discipline.

Fearful of what they might do to us, I pondered leaving but didn't want to break my commitment.

The man stood in the center of our giant circle and asked us to be silent. When the last whisper had faded away, he spoke.

"Shortly, you will enter the meditation room. Please take

care of any needs before you enter, and do so quickly. If you have any medical needs, please see Amia, the nurse."

They have a nurse?

"And please remain silent."

One woman burst out laughing, and he spun around to face her.

"This isn't funny," he admonished. "This is about your life. Please pay attention to my instructions and prepare to take yourself very seriously. If you're not ready to take yourself seriously, then leave."

Another young woman ran out of the room crying, followed by one of the staff.

"All right," he resumed, "I assume the rest of you are here to stay. Be ready to begin in ten minutes."

People began to scurry around. Some went to the restroom; others talked to Amia or refilled their water bottles. I couldn't help wondering what had happened to that woman who had run out.

Then I saw Amia wrapping an Ace bandage around someone's leg. I couldn't imagine why, but then I thought about how my knees had given out in the past and wondered if I should get wrapped too. Then I thought perhaps my brief time should be used to go to the restroom again, so I chose the latter.

When we reassembled, a beautiful but somber woman in a long black dress emerged. I wondered if she would be the one to set me free.

"It's time," she announced.

She and the man opened the double doors, revealing the main room.

My heart was pounding. I felt a sudden surge of energy rush through my body as I glanced around the meditation room we were now assembled in—a huge ballroom with green carpeting and a disco ball hanging from the ceiling—which was guarded by people clad in all black, a stark contrast from the white walls and bright lights. I shivered from the cranked-up air-conditioning.

On a platform in the back of the room stood a group of people who looked like angels in their simple, flowing clothes in light colors. They appeared to be glowing from the inside, much like Teri had been when I last saw her. They focused directly on us in such a soft and caring way that it took my breath away. I felt their silent honoring of us for showing up, for being willing to take a deep look at ourselves.

Suddenly, nothing else mattered. Everything I had gone through to get to this point had been worth it. The obstacles, the worries, the doubts, the fears. I knew I was exactly where I was supposed to be.

Multiple groupings of ten chairs in horseshoe shapes were set up around the massive room. There was a guide standing in front of each grouping who held a sign bearing that group's corresponding number. A woman in the center of the room spoke through a microphone, her voice deep and purposeful as though giving directions to a passel of unruly children.

"Please find the group corresponding to the number on your nametag," she instructed. "No more hanging out with the people you know. You are all individuals, equals, on a journey together that is about to unfold. When you find your group, take a chair and put your belongings under it, then close your eyes and sit in silence."

I found my group number and took a seat, taking a quick survey around to see whom I had ended up with. Sheila was not in my group, nor was Jim, nor the cute guy I'd been eyeing from across the room.

When we had all settled in our chairs, the woman in the center of the room spoke again. She had not introduced herself to us yet, but she was obviously our leader. When I opened my eyes briefly to look at her, she reminded me of my first grade teacher. She was stunningly beautiful, and I was afraid to do anything wrong in her presence.

"You have all been through a lot to get here," she said. "Now it's time to make the commitment to finish this workshop, and to do whatever it takes to get to the other side of the issues you came here to heal." She slowly scanned the room. "It's not going to be easy for any of you. You all have a lot to face. Right now I want you to open your eyes, and I want each of you to stand up in front of your respective group members and tell the others exactly how you feel."

She held up her index finger in a meaningful gesture.

"And the rest of you, if you don't feel that the person talking is telling the truth, I want you to let them know that. Don't let them sit down until they have told the truth. Understood?"

Heads nodded.

In some ways, this reminded me of being in the therapy group with Seth and my ex-sister-in-law, Evelyn, where I was afraid of being confronted if people felt I was holding back.

"Okay. Begin. Don't wait. Don't be the last one. Get up and tell the truth."

I sat in my chair, paralyzed, as the others in my circle stood up, one after another.

One angry man got up and insisted that he should never have come and that he wanted to leave. No one in the group believed him, and he was asked by the group leader to remain standing until he could tell us the truth. Then he broke down. Seeing him so raw, I recalled all the times I had accused men of being devoid of feeling. I melted in empathy for him.

One woman tried to hide behind a mask of giggles, skirting the issues of her life, unable to take responsibility for any of her own actions. She appeared nervous, but she also seemed to not be taking the process seriously. She told us she was a mom, and she couldn't understand why her children didn't respect her and why her husband left her for a younger woman. She said everything in a way that made her sound like a victim.

Unlike how I felt about the angry man from moments before, I couldn't empathize with her.

"No room for that here," someone in our group shouted. "Who are you, really?"

"We want to know what's really going on with you!" yelled another.

The woman reminded me of my mother. I felt like slapping her and imploring her to wake up.

Then it was my turn.

Like a trapped rat, I looked around for an escape, but there was no one else left. Everyone had shared except me, and they all sat staring at me, their faces open with anticipation. I knew I had to get up, or ... what?

Overcome with shame, I rose to my feet and somehow found myself in front of the group. I tried to make eye contact with them, but blood was rushing to my face and I knew I was turning red. I looked down at my shoes. Rubbing my sweaty palms together, I fought the urge to flee.

They're probably noticing how old I am, how short, how insecure. Why didn't I wear a different T-shirt? These shoes are dirty. I shouldn't be here.

I stood frozen, unable to utter a word.

The designated leader of our group was a woman and her shrill voice shook me out of my paralysis. She had been the one to instruct the angry man to remain standing until he could share his real truth. She paced behind the chairs of our horseshoe, and I could sense her eyes boring through the back of my head.

"Jan, stop the bullshit and get real," she snapped.

"I'm trying to be real," I insisted.

But I could tell no one believed me.

"Don't try. Just be real. We want to know who you are," shouted one of the women in the group, obviously spurred on by the leader's approach.

I took a deep breath. "I want you to know who I am," I said in a shaky voice. "*I* want to know who I am. That's why I'm here."

A man seated next to me looked up at me intently and said, "So why are you so angry? Why are you blaming us for not understanding you? How can we know you if you don't show us who you are?" He sounded accusatory.

"I don't have anything more to say," I replied flatly.

Another man asked, "Why not? What are you here for? And why do you have that angry look on your face?"

Angry look? I wasn't aware of any angry look.

A young woman with a softer, more compassionate voice asked, "Don't you want to get to the truth?"

I was struggling to be real, but I wasn't sure what that meant. The façade that had held me together in my life was useless here. Every time I opened my mouth, I found myself confronted by human mirrors, believing they simply didn't get me.

Not wanting to admit to my own anger, I judged them. But they kept demanding more of me. There was nowhere to run, and these people were relentless.

I finally felt myself begin to weaken. When I let go of my pride and judgment, I could truly see for a moment—see that they cared and did want to know me.

Feeling overwhelmed, I suddenly let out a loud scream and my body went rigid. Someone came up and embraced me gently from behind as I felt my knees buckling, berating myself for not being able to express myself with honesty.

I heard a gentle voice saying to me, "Open your eyes, Jan, and look at each person in the group."

The voice came from our group leader, the same woman who had yelled at me to get real.

Looking around, I saw eyes filled with love and compassion and I connected with them. The walls were down.

The angel embracing me from behind guided me to a place on the floor, where I sat frozen, like a caged animal set free, unable to decide what to do next as music began to pulsate throughout the room. It was a song I had heard before but never felt this deeply: the Doors' "Break On Through to the Other Side." It vibrated through my body as I began to move.

At that point, everyone else was directed by the beautiful woman with the microphone to find a place on the floor as well.

Did I start this? I wondered. *Are they all feeling like me?*

I began screaming again, and someone handed me a big pillow and a plastic bat to hit it with. I focused all my hate on the pillow and let myself swing, just like I'd done previously in therapy.

"I hate my life!" *Whap!*

"I hate my father for expecting me to be perfect and for causing me to feel so much shame." *Whap!*

"I hate Joel for cheating on me." *Whap!*

"I hate Rocko for manipulating me." *Whap!*

"I hate Seth for using me when I needed help." *Whap!*

"I hate Rick for slapping me around." *Whap!*

"Mom—" I stopped for a moment. "I can't hate my mom. I love her. But she didn't show me how to take care of myself, dammit!" *Whap!*

"I hate that people don't get me." *Whap!*

I saw images of everyone who had hurt me, of every person

who had let me down. I cried and repeatedly beat that pillow until I fell to the floor, exhausted.

When I became more conscious of what was going on around me, I noticed hard rock music playing loudly, filling the room with permission to let the rage out.

People were yelling in various languages, and some of them were crying, pounding the floor, the walls, and the pillows. Everyone was letting go.

My mind raced so fast I couldn't keep track. Panicky, I scanned the room and fell into my familiar pattern. *Where's that guy? The cute one with the curly hair? I wonder if he's attracted to me. Maybe I can lean on him. Maybe he'll help me through this.*

I did my best to get my bearings, but there was nothing to anchor me. I was trembling, wondering if I found my true love, if everything would be okay.

Hours seemed to pass as I lay on the floor.

Then, the leader returned to the center again and announced that we were finished in that room for the day. She reminded us to stay deep and focused and silent as we drove back to the hotel. She added that she wanted us to be clear and well rested for the day ahead. Just when I couldn't imagine it getting more intense, she told us we had homework—we had to write about our families, our desires, our painful experiences, what we wanted from this Intensive, and what we really cared about. As exhausted as I was, I was excited about delving even deeper into myself. I had hope that the workshop would help me get to the bottom of who I really was, and I was going to follow all instructions closely to ensure I was successful.

I could still feel the Doors' song reverberating through me, making me feel ready to "break on through to the other side," as I embarked on my homework that night. Struggling to stay awake long enough to finish it, I was determined to get it right. My two roommates had turned off their lights long before and were sleeping soundly when I eventually fell into a deep, peaceful sleep.

17

MORE LETTING GO

THE MORNING PROGRAM AT THE CENTER PUSHED US deeper into telling the truth about our lives, and I was overcome with love and respect as I watched my fellow workshop participants bare their innermost secrets in front of one another. My sense of compassion was at an all-time high and I was feeling more comfortable about opening up.

We took a noon break and ate a meager lunch of rice and tofu in silence, then followed our leaders back into the meditation room, where we sat on the floor and watched a progression of traumatic pictures on a movie screen: people who were suffering, dying, starving, or tortured, and people who had limited options in life. Vulnerable as we were from our experience of baring our souls, it wasn't long before most of us were in tears.

I fought crying, but to no avail. The pain bubbled up from a place deep inside, so deep that I had never dared to let myself go there before. I cried for the people in the images we'd seen on the screen, for the people there in the room, for my family, for the world.

I cried for myself.

Eventually, through the tears, all the judgment I had felt faded away and only the pain remained. I saw pictures in my mind of Dad biting his lip, exploding, storming through the house, intent on punishing one of us for doing something wrong. We didn't deserve to be hurt, but Dad turned into a monster, unable to contain his own rage. It made me wonder: Did Dad have pain too? Was he afraid of his father like we were of him? Did he get beaten? I had heard him say his father was strict. Maybe he endured painful punishments too. None of us, not even him, deserved to be treated that way.

It wasn't until almost midnight that we walked out of the room in silence. Together, we were all coming to know a higher degree of compassion. We were told that there was more to come, that we would continue to go deeper, that we would discover more profound levels of compassion, that we would surrender even further.

Despite the long, emotional day, I wasn't at all tired. Instead I felt restless, open, and vulnerable. After doing my writing for the night, I headed to the hotel's outdoor hot tub to relax and assimilate, only to discover I wasn't the only one with that idea.

The cute, curly-haired guy was there, surrounded by women and flirting shamelessly.

Hoping no one would look at my body, I slipped quickly into the warm water. There, safely under the blanket of bubbles, my self-consciousness evaporated, and I let the water carry me easily, laughing as I bumped into one welcoming body after another.

"Hey there," he said as I bumped into him.

"Hi," I said, and smiled.

He turned toward me and I floated into his arms. It was exciting and sexual, and I had no desire to push him away.

After introducing himself as Gary, the rules about staying

deep and focused and abstaining from sexual contact flashed through my mind. But I convinced myself that I needed this—I needed to feel attractive and desirable.

Long after everyone else had left the hot tub, Gary and I remained. I relished the sweet nothings he whispered in my ear. "Where have you been?" "You're so beautiful." We had easy conversation about a multitude of topics. He said his last girlfriend didn't want to take the same kind of vacations he did. He liked adventurous ones. So did I. He said he liked to feel independent while in a relationship. So did I. That night in the warm water, we seemed like a perfect match.

Delightful waves of sensual energy surged through me, out-of-control bursts that made me want to let go entirely and let him have me. I knew he was feeling it too because when I was wrapped around his body, I could feel every part of him.

It was close to dawn when Gary walked me to my room and kissed me, a lingering, romantic kiss that stayed with me. After he left, it was hours before my excitement died down. I finally drifted off to sleep barely before it was time to get up for the next day of activities.

When I arrived for the silent breakfast, I caught sight of Gary sitting at a table with several women, making what appeared to be deep eye contact with one, then with another. Convinced that I was the special one, I shrugged it off, thinking, *Why else would he have spent so much intimate time with me last night?*

MIDWAY THROUGH THE WEEK, I APPROACHED GARY AGAIN after breakfast on a day when we had the morning free to do what we wanted, a break from the rigid structure we had all been following.

"Got any plans for this morning?" I asked him.

He shrugged. "I'm not sure yet what I'm going to do."

"Oh," I said, trying to sound nonchalant while my knees shook. "I'm going to do some laundry, and then go for a walk."

"Great! I'll join you," he said. "I'll go get my laundry and we can do it together."

With a spring in my step, I rushed to my room to get my dirty clothes, then headed to the laundry area. As I was sorting my clothes, Gary sauntered in and dropped his bag of laundry on the floor.

"I've decided I want to go with some people to the beach," he said. "You don't mind throwing in a few of my things with your wash, do you?"

I stood there speechless for a moment. "No, that's fine," I stammered, "I don't mind."

He gave me a quick peck on the cheek and dashed out the door with a wave of his hand.

But I did mind. While I disparaged myself for not having the courage to say it to his face, I couldn't help but wonder why I kept letting this happen. Instead of owning my insecurity, I poured extra bleach on one of his shirts, convinced it was his fault that my day was ruined.

Later, as we assembled for the afternoon session, I saw Gary laughing with some other people and felt the heat rise in my face. I was angry that he wasn't taking the retreat seriously, yet at the same time I longed for him to notice me, to laugh with me, to continue the intimacy that had felt like the beginning of a beautiful relationship.

In the meditation room we were asked to choose a partner. I looked for Gary, but after seeing that one of his female beach buddies had already paired up with him, I panicked. I needed a good partner, someone who knew me and with whom I felt comfortable. Just then, a random woman appeared who needed a partner too. My anxiety lessened a bit as

I gave her a perfunctory smile and she returned it, eyes downcast with her own apparent unease.

We were instructed to gaze silently at each other, and I immediately sensed pain and discomfort emanating from her.

Oh my God, I thought, she's just like me.

She shared her story, confiding in me about her love for a man who wanted nothing more to do with her, the trouble she was having letting go, and how she wanted to be in a normal relationship and feel good again.

I felt a kinship with her. And even better, I found some solace in realizing I wasn't alone in my dysfunction.

THE NEXT FEW DAYS OF THE INTENSIVE WERE LIKE A blur. One day melted into the next as we followed orders, took breaks to eat, sleep, and use the restroom, and were instructed to drop to the floor again and again, to fall into our feelings and focus on being in the moment. The beautiful female leader—who called herself Lady Mary—spoke to us often from the center of the room, gently encouraging us to let go, to let God take us.

"Don't give up," she urged. "Don't let the fear stop you. How much time do you think you have?" She crooned on and on hypnotically. "Don't hold back a thing. Give it all to God. You deserve to be loved."

As her voice would melt away, heavy metal rock music swelled in every corner of the room.

Finding my own rhythm in this playpen of freedom, I was expressing myself in ways that normally would elicit judgment, punishment, and pain. Anger surged through my body, energy I could now express openly here, as I screamed my pain, thinking, *How could Gary have treated me so badly? Damn him! Why did I let him do that to me?*

I realized in this exercise that holding my feelings inside was a prison for me. As I sensed walls closing in on me with escalating rage that was strong enough to make me danger-ous, I felt the urge to destroy everything in my way.

This must be how Dad felt when he lost control.

Moving around on the floor like a baby, I let my body guide me through this struggle for life, my life, facing the de-mons that kept me trapped in my own body. I kept my eyes closed to keep my focus internal. I had committed to do what-ever it took to get free, and I had to allow the monster within me to emerge.

My clothes were suddenly in the way and inhibition gave way. Others were disrobing too, and I no longer felt the need to hide.

Off came the shirt.

I need to be free. Get me out of here.

I felt I was being held against a wall, just like when Rick hit me. I saw Dad biting his lip and coming toward me.

The assistants I called angels were there for us as we let go, keeping us safe, praying for us. One of them handed me a glass of water and touched me gently to let me know I was not alone.

As power surged through my body with the courage and the strength to fight for myself, I was unstoppable. The angels prepared a safe place for me to let it all out by placing mat-tresses and pillows all around me, surprisingly aware of where I might go next.

Using energy I had held back for so many years, I punched and kicked and moved like a wild animal wherever my body took me. The images of the abusers were coming forward and I was poised to annihilate them. I had been the victim. Now I was the conqueror.

One of the angels whispered in my ear, "Keep going, Jan. Don't give up. You're worth it."

Just then, an energy bigger and more benevolent than any concept of God I had ever encountered pervaded the room. Feeling connected with everyone yet still free to be in my own space, I released a blood-curdling scream from deep within. I was exhausted but refused to rest, pushing harder, as if I were giving birth to myself while deep guttural moans poured out of me.

Then, eyes still closed, I saw a dark, ominous form in front of me. "No! Stop it!" I yelled in a voice that was louder and more assertive than I'd ever heard from myself before.

With newfound strength, I saw myself as a baby, crying out for help. I picked myself up and comforted this baby version of me, protecting my innocence. I gasped and then breathed a sigh of relief.

I am safe now. This can never happen to me again.

The quiet voice then came to me, the one inside that had been there all along, sweetly echoing my truth. I relaxed and lay flat on the floor, arms and legs spread out comfortably, feeling the support of the floor beneath me and the loving energy in the room.

In that position, my body began to move in harmony with my own energy, my pelvis shifting rhythmically up and down. This freedom of movement was reminiscent of intense moments of ecstasy. I felt safe, connected with God, determined to hold back nothing. I wasn't sure where I had been or why it had taken me so long to get here, but I had finally made it and there was nothing to fear.

When I opened my eyes to see what was happening around me, I saw a woman dancing to the erotic music that filled the air. She had no partner, nor did she need one. Watching her, I felt my own body gyrating and stood up, finding my own rhythm. Unhindered by the reservations and restrictions of my past, I screamed, "God!" as I had so many times while making love, but never quite like this. All the love

I had held back came storming through, breaking down the barriers that had kept me from myself. Natural and free, my body danced and swayed as though I'd been there all my life.

Spent at last, I fell to the floor, in love with everyone and everything.

As I lay on the floor in complete stillness, my body trembling with the fullness of freed energy, I was filled with gratitude for this amazing opportunity.

This must be God, I thought. *Heaven on earth.*

After hours and hours of labor, I was finally fully present and calm.

When I opened my eyes, I found myself looking at Lady Mary, who was kneeling beside me. She was beautiful, loving, and accepting, reflecting back to me my own loving presence. Feeling no separation, I felt safe with my beloved self and everyone else, all of us now one moving organism with individual reflections.

A gentle stranger, angelic and strong, then tenderly lifted me to my feet and took me to join others who were celebrating their freedom. Brimming with joy, I passed by the good-looking man from the intro session I had attended weeks ago, the one who said I castrated men. He was cheering me on.

Those celebrating were gathered in a circle in the center of the room as angelic music played, filling my entire being. I danced as I had never danced before, surrounded by people who knew me as no one ever had. When the dancing ended, one of the angels led me to a mirror in a corner of the room.

"Look at yourself, Jan," she said.

I froze for an instant. Rarely had I approved of my image in the mirror, but I found the courage to look and saw my eyes shining back at me, clear and beautiful, my face aglow. This was the real me. I was beautiful, sexy, free, and passionate.

Divine me.

LATER, IN MY HOTEL ROOM, I FOUND JIM LYING ON ONE of the beds. Ever so gently, I stretched out beside him. We exchanged a loving hug and fell asleep in each other's arms. When Sheila came in a little later and draped herself on the other side of him, it was as if the three of us had become one body.

As new questions presented themselves to me, I didn't try to figure out the answers. I was confident that love would show me the way.

18

GOD'S LOVER

*T*HE NEXT DAY, BACK IN THE INTENSIVE ARENA, THE
feeling of excitement was titillating and I could feel a
woman's presence before she walked in. Beautiful and vibrant, her mere existence transfigured the room. I hadn't seen
her before, but she smiled in recognition of the human angels
and some of the participants who obviously knew who she was.

"Who's that?" I asked one of the staff members sitting
next to me.

"That's Kali," she whispered, "the wife of the man who
started this whole thing, the man who broke free first."

The man's voice on the tape.

I remembered hearing their story from Teri. Sam and his
wife Becky were both devoted to finding God in their lives.
Dissatisfied with the usual religions and rituals they had experienced, they prayed and prayed, devoting their lives to the
search for God. When Becky had a child, she became more
focused on being a mother, yet she and Sam never gave up
their search for God. They discovered that music took them
deeper, and that became their outlet of expressing themselves
freely to the Divine. As they allowed for this new understanding and their bodies opened up, they came to realize for them-

selves that God was inside of their beings. Like gravity, God's presence was what held everything together.

Sam's transformation began to take on a life of its own. He said another being, which his followers believed was an incarnation of God, benevolently possessed him. Sam agreed to give up his life as he knew it, surrendering to this being. His body began to change form and he spoke with such wisdom, understanding, and love that people believed his presence to be that of God himself.

As the story goes, Sam's body couldn't handle all the energy that was flowing through him and he died of unknown causes. After his passing, Becky was inspired to take the name Kali, the name of a Hindu goddess associated with empowerment. She claimed to be the "voice of God" and said she was channeling the one who took over her husband's body. As is often the case when a master dies, the energy in the group expanded and could no longer be supported by Kali alone.

Thus, Angels of God was created, and intensives, like the one I was attending, were drawing in more and more believers. Truthfully, the story of how the group came to be scared me a little, and I wondered if my body would give out like Sam's if I continued on this path.

In that moment, though, I was in awe. Kali was so free with her body that she was glowing as she sat in an oversized chair in the front of the room, surrounded by beautiful flowers. There were two women kneeling beside her, anticipating her every need. One offered her water but she pushed it away, staying focused on us.

"I want to thank you all, each and every one of you, for your courage," she said, looking around the room. "And now comes the real test of your courage. Will you really do anything for God? What steps are you ready to take to keep your connection, and to keep your heart open?"

Anything, of course, I thought. Then I wondered what God, working through Kali, would ask me to do next.

Kali began calling out our names, putting us into groups. Mine consisted of ten women—"God's Lovers," she called us. We were told that we were to prepare ourselves for a date with God and to remain in silence until noon the following day.

We were all a bit mystified, but in our state of openness accepted that somehow everything would unfold in perfect order, as it had during this entire experience. We were then given the names of nearby stores and directed to go shopping for the occasion. Our job was to follow our hearts in search of an outfit that would allow our "true selves" to come through, and we were specifically told to be "sexy" for God. It felt exciting, like I was preparing for a date with a man I'd already had sex with.

The retail stores they sent us to were specifically for lingerie, and we weren't given much time. I had never liked lingerie and never made an effort to wear it for any man, yet now I was expected to wear it for God?

As we shopped, it angered me that some of my silent sisters were so brazen, choosing sexy pieces they were used to wearing for their lovers. I couldn't help but wonder why I had to do all this for God. Didn't He love me the way I was?

Fighting old internal programming that told me I looked fat and sloppy in seductive finery, I struggled to make a choice. Finally, with the help of a couple of my silent cohorts (although I confess to some muffled giggling and whispering), I picked out a black lace teddy and a silky see-through robe. I bartered with my inner critic by rationalizing that I could keep the robe and use it for another occasion sometime in the future.

We stayed up late that night pampering ourselves. We did each other's nails and exchanged massages, enjoying the sensuality of our beings. There was no tension in the air as sometimes exists when women compete for a man's attention. We were preparing ourselves for God and He loved us all. How could there be competition? God had shown me how inclusive He was, not leaving anyone out.

And so I trusted.

That night I fell into my usual deep sleep as I had experienced every night during the Intensive.

I WOKE UP TO A GENTLE KNOCK ON THE DOOR.

"It's time," a voice said.

We congregated in one room and got ready. I let two women help me with my makeup and hair, and when I looked in the mirror, I saw that I was indeed beautiful, as much as the day of my breakthrough.

This was for God.

It still wasn't clear what we were supposed to do as we gathered in the parking lot to travel to the Center. The sight of all of us standing in the parking lot in our respective groups was surreal. There were clusters dressed as monks, waitresses, police officers, hippies, and nuns—and then there were the ten of us bundled up in robes to conceal our scantily clad bodies.

The meditation room was festive with flowers and banners and the angels were already seated. I took a seat with my group in the large circle of chairs, appreciating the radiance of each of my sisters. Though feeling beautiful, I was still quite nervous, hardly ready to share this much of myself with the whole group. Yes, I had done it in my breakthrough, but this felt different somehow.

There were people in the room I hadn't seen before, but it was clear they had done the Intensive. As the room buzzed with voices and laughter, my body was shivering.

"Who wants to go first?" Kali asked.

Not me. Don't pick me.

Hands went up and Lady Mary walked toward the group of men dressed as monks.

"Are you ready?" She asked each of them, one at a time.

Some said yes right away while others seemed apprehensive, so she counseled each of them to allay their fears. After some time, Lady Mary called them to the center of the room to the accompaniment of perfectly timed soothing music, the kind you hear when getting a massage. She leaned in and whispered something to each one individually, and they began to move around the room as if in a trance.

The music suddenly switched to sexy beats with provocative words, and they started to dance as though possessed, freely moving their bodies like rock stars, gyrating around the room wildly without inhibition. We all stood up and clapped, supporting them in their expression, as if moved by that unseen benevolent force that had been with us all week.

As they grooved around the room, connecting with everyone, their monk robes slipped off. Even the shyest among them was prancing now, spirituality meeting sexuality in a way that honored the energy of God in all of us.

They continued to whirl around as three or four more sexy songs were played, again perfectly timed. And then "Hero" by Mariah Carey came on—a slow song about finding your strength inside—at which point the group of men fell to the floor in surrender, completely used up by the force that had taken them over and moved them to express their true selves.

I became apprehensive again as Lady Mary scanned the room. She chose one group after another until my lingerie-clad sisters and I were the only ones left. When she motioned us to come to the center of the room, I clutched my robe around myself, hoping I could keep it on, that no one would notice the imperfections of my body.

I heard Lady Mary whisper in my ear, "Jan, you're beautiful. Show God how much you love Him. You've held back your whole life. It's time to let go."

It was her energy, as much as her words and her sweet yet powerful voice, that reached deep into my soul and liberated me.

"I Would Do Anything for Love" by Meat Loaf began to play, and I let go, forgetting my shame, my insecurities, and my guilt. Then, more erotic music flowed through the air and gave me some sort of permission to move my body like a seductress, gyrating my pelvis freely, swinging my arms, bending this way and that in the large circle of love.

I danced for God, for everyone there, for myself. Focused on no one in particular and yet connecting with everyone, I noticed the other members of my group doing the same, touching hands, hearts open.

After a few minutes, the robe became more of a hindrance than something to hide behind, so I let it fall to the floor. Wearing nothing but a flimsy black teddy, near naked in front of hundreds of people, I danced with a few chosen men who ran into the circle to join us. It felt like a perfect expression of God's unconditional love.

After a number of songs, the mood slowly shifted, and the forgiving sounds of "Amazing Grace" filled the room. We all dropped to the floor in exhaustion as the lights were dimmed and the angels gently covered us with blankets. At one point, I opened my eyes and looked up at the glittery disco ball high above. *I will never forget*, I thought with deep gratitude.

I DECIDED TO STAY AN EXTRA NIGHT BEFORE RETURNING to my everyday life, and a man with whom I connected during the week suggested I stay with him. I wasn't attracted to him physically, but I felt safe with him, so I agreed.

We spent the evening sharing our deepest thoughts and personal experiences we'd had the past few days, and he gave me a foot massage filled with deep love and compassion that I will always remember. By the morning's light, I knew I was going to savor the past week's divine quality with passion and deep appreciation for the rest of my life.

But I wasn't sure how this newfound energy I was experiencing was going to work back at home. Some things, I knew, were going to have to change.

19

⌗

THE ROAD HOME

*F*AMILIAR WITH THE TRANSITION I WOULD BE GOING through after the Intensive, Teri invited me to stop by her place on my way home. Her life had changed since she had attended hers: she was living in a retreat center, in a community environment with natural hot springs.

During our visit, she gently guided me through a day of soaking in the healing waters, eating a healthy dinner in the community dining room, and then tucking me into a single bed in a small room with a view of beautiful trees and mountains in the distance. I slept like a baby.

The next day as I prepared to go home—or to the place I had been living before the Intensive—I realized that home now meant something a lot deeper to me than just a physical place.

SOON AFTER MY RETURN, I HAD DINNER WITH CHRISTINE. Unable to contain my fervor from the retreat—my voice was actually still hoarse from all the letting go—I bubbled over with enthusiasm for my newly discovered path, positive that she would want to hear about it and that she would be intrigued. Despite being asked to keep details about the Intensive confidential, I told her about the angels and Kali and the amazing new friends I had found.

"You really should do this too," I said. "You won't believe how it will change your life."

She waited until I paused to take a breath, and then, in her usual deliberate manner, she said, "Jan, I think you'd better be careful. This sounds like a cult to me. It could be dangerous. Please be careful. You sound like you took a drug or something, like you drank the Kool-Aid, if you know what I mean."

"No, it's not like that at all," I said. I didn't want to come across as defensive, but it was too late. I had an agenda, and Christine was not buying it.

"I feel like you're preaching at me," she said, "like this is the only way or something."

I didn't want her to be right, so I convinced myself that she simply didn't understand. Maybe if she did the Intensive, I reasoned, she would get it. But I was pretty certain that wasn't going to happen.

After that dinner, I knew I needed to get beyond Christine's judgment and allow myself to feel the pain of it. This was what the Intensive had taught me. But Linda, another one of my friends, had also made an abrupt exit from my life, suggesting that my spiritual healing was a cult before I could share much about my experience. When I talked about the Intensive with my sister Lynn, showing her a picture of Kali, she too pulled back.

"She's scary," Lynn said.

My first thought was, *How dare she talk about my spiritual master that way!* But then I tried to explain who Kali was to me, that she was the freest, most fulfilled person I had ever been with.

But Lynn didn't buy it.

"Why do you do all this stuff, Jan? Why can't you just live your life and be happy? Get over it. It's time to move on."

After Lynn's response, I continued to retreat within myself. I didn't want to feel separate from my sister, or from anyone else in my life, but I was baffled as to why they didn't get my transformation. I knew they could all benefit from what I'd gone through; I reasoned that they simply weren't ready to be that raw, to let go, to take off the masks. I wanted to help them evolve the way I had, but a nagging voice kept assaulting me:

What if they're right? What if this whole thing was a waste of time and I should just forget it and live a normal life, like them?

I abruptly stopped as I caught myself hanging onto my old ways of denial, resentment, and judgment. I had a choice now, and I was determined to find a way to live in integrity and love, to learn to have compassion for others as well as myself, to feel the ecstasy I experienced after my breakthrough and my let-go dance.

Seeking acceptance for my newfound perspective, I shared my experience with Mom. I knew she didn't quite understand, but she listened, and she seemed happy for me. No, she didn't get it—or get me—the way I wished, but at least there was no resistance.

Convinced I had no one in my outside world who truly knew me, I began to depend on those I'd met at the Intensive as my lifeline, as the source of my connection to God. I believed it was the group and the process that would allow me to keep going, to stay focused, to fend off the illusion, so I chose to leave my small apartment at my parents' house and move in with two people I had met at the Intensive, Cathy and Jose.

Encouraged by Kali as a part of the process, others from the Intensive were moving in together as well; living in small groups with like-minded people would give us an opportunity to support one another in our love and devotion to God. I had never had much support for my spiritual path before, so moving in with people who had done the Intensive was like a dream come true. Now I could commune daily with those who were in alignment with the direction I wanted to take.

But while it was good for me to be around people on a similar spiritual path, I quickly learned that living with other people, whether from the Intensive or not, would always present challenges and continued learning opportunities.

One evening Jose walked into the living room naked, declaring that it was important for him to be able to be unclothed at home. Cathy seemed fine with this, or at least willing to let Jose have his way. But I was shocked; in fact, if I had been honest, I would have shared how disrespected I felt. Instead, I fell back into my old pattern of being the pleasant, nice girl on the exterior, claiming to be fine with it, while seething inside.

My integrity was slipping.

Connecting with my truth, I knew I didn't find it acceptable for others to run around naked in my home. But this meant facing the challenge of telling Jose. It also meant being open to everything that followed.

I approached him one night and told him I needed to talk to him about something.

"Sure, sweetie, what is it?"

"Well, this is hard to say, but the other night when you were naked, I wanted to be okay with it, but, well, it's really not okay with me."

He registered a look of shock, then instead of talking to me about it, stormed out of the room. As I sat wondering what to do next, I heard him screaming into a towel and pacing the floor in the other room.

Awhile later, he returned.

"Okay, Jan. I understand," he said calmly. "But I would like to be able to be naked in my area of the house."

"Okay," I conceded, "that's fine. Just not in the common areas."

He agreed, and I felt a tiny spark of victory that I had been able to speak my truth. My internal power source was growing. But the uphill climb toward total harmony was only beginning.

EVERY DAY IN OUR HOME PRESENTED A NEW SET OF CHAL-lenges I couldn't anticipate.

One day, for example, I walked into the kitchen to fix myself something to eat while Jose was cooking his dinner. When Cathy walked in, she said something to Jose that triggered him, and they began yelling at each another. Caught in the crossfire, I tensed up. Their anger and expressiveness scared me so I left the house. When I came home, Cathy confronted me.

"Jan, you're so passive. I'm so angry with you. Why did you just walk out on us like that?"

"Because you were yelling at each other."

"So why didn't you say something if we were bothering you?"

"I was about to, but you guys were yelling so loud that I had to get away."

"That's what you always do, Jan. You run away." Her voice escalated. "Why don't you stick around and tell us how you're feeling instead of running away? What's wrong with you?"

I immediately felt overpowered and wanted to flee again, but since she was upset with me for doing that in the first place, I stayed.

"I'm so sorry," I sobbed. "It's hard for me to express myself."

Knowing I couldn't suppress my frustration, I ran into the living room, put on some music, and screamed as I danced to get the energy out. Eventually, Cathy and I were able to talk things out. Even though I was still feeling defensive inside, I was proud that I was finally learning how to stand up for myself, and how to handle the emotions that used to leave me feeling depressed and throwing daggers.

My biggest realization at that time was how comfortable I was as a victim; I also deeply desired to stop languishing in that role, while fearing the power of my own emotions. My father frequently lost control by expressing rage, and I had learned from Mom, who had constantly buried her feelings to avoid confronting Dad, to turn my anger in on myself to keep from inflicting it on others. Reflecting on that natural reaction, I discovered that these behaviors I had learned early on were a form of survival; they had become a part of me before I was making conscious decisions. Although they were still causing me pain, I had learned at the Intensive it was in the pain that I could find healing. The problem was that the only way out was to go deeper into the pain. Despite the fact that this was not going to be an easy or quick way to find my true self, I resolved to trust the process, keep going, and not let the fear stop me.

20

⁂

LIVING THE DREAM

*D*URING THIS TIME IN MY LIFE, JOSE, CATHY, AND I would host gatherings on a regular basis, and about ten of us would regularly meet to meditate and confront one another's illusions and façades. It was the way we had learned to help each other face the dark side of ourselves, the part we couldn't see but that those who loved us saw so clearly.

Our house had a huge living room and we chose to leave it empty so we would have the space to meditate the way we did at the Intensive. After confronting one another, we would do a deep meditation with one person coordinating the music we had heard at the Intensive, driving us deeper and deeper within. Toward the end of the three-hour meditation, the music would turn to joyful dance tunes and we would celebrate. On one occasion, as "Sing Hallelujah" blasted through the house, we all ran out into the yard impulsively, bursting with glee and sharing the freedom of letting go.

To further our growth, we each committed to exploring specific practices that would stretch us and help us free ourselves from our illusions. Unlike my Catholic experiences, I felt a sense of freedom to choose to do or not do what I had committed to without guilt. For instance, at some point I decided not to eat sugar, and because I was so used to disciplining myself, I rigidly refused anything that had sugar in it. Yes, I was honoring my promise to myself, but I also felt incredibly deprived. Then someone in the group suggested that maybe I would feel freer if I didn't follow all the rules all of the time. And guess what? I found the one piece of chocolate that broke my sugar fast to be ecstatically delicious and mentally freeing. Even more, it was okay to not be so rigid and to even make mistakes. In fact, it made me see that mistakes were a way of showing us how human we all are.

Living a life that was intertwined with those from the Intensive, I felt an acceptance from them—and from within myself—that I had never experienced before. I had longed for a community like this my whole life, and I hoped it would last forever. Despite being different ages, from varied backgrounds, and having disparate careers, we were all committed to following this path to freedom, convinced it was the only way.

One day Kali, through her messengers, contacted everyone in the organization and directed us to come to San Diego that night for a "special meditation." Without hesitation, Cathy, Jose, and I dropped everything and rearranged our schedules so we could be there. My expectations of what "special" meant propelled me forward, leaving any discernment locked in the back of my mind.

Could this be it? I wondered. *Is this the night I'll become completely free?*

The room was filled with hundreds of people, and we swayed as one body, arms high in the air, propelled by seductive music. Some cried out as we surrendered to the energy in the room. It was as if God was calling us home through Kali. Tingling in anticipation of her entrance, I blended into the wave that flowed through the room ... yet something felt off.

Recently, my internal voice had started picking up on the growing inconsistencies in Kali's group, and I wondered if it was just me. The Intensive had been all about my personal freedom, letting go, working through family issues, and coping in the world. It had been a huge breakthrough for me to confront these elements of my life, and I was hopeful the results would stay with me always. I was so happy and relieved to live with people who felt the same way that they became everything to me. They kept me real and authentic. They were my family.

But things were changing. The road to freedom, as laid out by our master, seemed to be narrowing. There were now rules to follow, rules that changed often, at Kali's whim. It was never questioned that she was already free and sourcing the will of God. Kali said she spoke for God, that she was the voice of God.

It seemed unorthodox to refute that until I flashed back to one of the reasons I left the Catholic Church: it was difficult for me to believe that the pope was infallible. Yet here we were, taking Kali's word as binding. She made decisions about where people should live and with whom; she sometimes split up couples, saying it was better for them to be apart. As we got closer to the center, and closer to Kali, more was demanded of us, including more and more money to sustain our spiritual life. People freely gave Kali things, such as houses, cars, and other necessities, which seemed okay to me at the time, since she was our master.

But then I began to wonder how far I would be willing to go, how much I could allow without seriously questioning the whole movement.

CATHY CAME RUNNING OUT OF HER ROOM, SHOUTING, "Kali's on the phone for us!"

Jose and I hurried to Cathy's room, and we listened for Kali's voice on the speakerphone as if we were listening for God, wondering if it was really Kali or if it was one of her assistants. But as soon as she spoke in her soft, melodic voice, asking if we were all there, we knew it was her. Shaking in anticipation of what she would ask of us, my eyes widened as I heard her say that if we wanted to stay on the serious path to God, we needed to move to San Diego as soon as possible and be near the Center.

And then her voice was gone.

It didn't take long before Cathy and Jose decided they would move to San Diego. Afraid of being left alone on the path, I began taking steps to relocate with them. But every step I took toward the move felt like walking in deep mud. Something simply didn't feel right to me.

Not only was I torn about picking up my life and relocating, but I'd noticed that some of the others in our group were showing up less frequently. Despite that observation, however, I told my law firm that I'd like a transfer from Los Angeles to their office in San Diego. But after my interview there, I discovered that I didn't feel comfortable in that office, and I realized that I didn't want to move so far away from my family.

Hopeful that Jose, Cathy, and I could still live together, I told them I'd decided to stay. But they had already found housing in San Diego that was approved by Kali.

Faced with giving up aspects of the path I had come to believe would lead me Home, I had to come to terms with the fact that moving was not a fit for me at that point. Could I move forward without the master and my friends and fellow angels close by? I wasn't sure, but I recalled what I'd heard Sam say on that cassette tape about following your inner pull, even if it's in a different direction from the organization or your spiritual master. A wave of relief flooded my body when I realized that even if I didn't move to San Diego, I could still meditate and make use of the practices I had learned. I had internalized the learnings I felt aligned within me. They were mine to keep.

CATHY, JOSE, AND I HAD BEEN LIVING TOGETHER FOR A year at that point, and it was difficult to say goodbye. On our last night as a trio, we did one final meditation, sitting on the floor and holding hands. Even though they wanted me to come with them, they accepted that I was going to stay in Los Angeles for now, hoping I would visit them in San Diego as often as possible.

Parting ways with them ripped my heart open, but I trusted that I was doing the right thing. Despite worrying that they might break free before I did—being part of the "special" group on a more serious path—I reveled in the fact that I didn't feel as alone as I had when others in my life had left me before. Even still, I perceived myself as on my own and moved in with my younger sister Lynn, feeling the need to be with someone I trusted.

I didn't see Cathy and Jose much after they left, except at some of the events I attended. When Cathy came to visit me a couple times, she talked incessantly of Kali and the path and all she was doing to free herself, continuing to speak of Kali as if she were God.

"So are you saying that if you left Kali and the group, you would be leaving God?" I asked her.

"Yes," she said without hesitation.

Her answer jolted me into realizing I had made the right decision by staying in Los Angeles. When Cathy admitted that she would do anything and go anywhere for Kali—for God—I began to see the group as my friends and family had seen it, like more of a cult. But in spite of that clarity, a pull still existed. At a certain point, when I was feeling alone and confused, still unsure about my decision to remain in Los Angeles, I decided to write Kali to see if she would provide some counsel for me.

> *Dear Kali,*
>
> *I was living in the Los Angeles group house with Cathy and Jose. As our master, you directed us to move to San Diego to be closer to you and the more serious followers. I intended to make that move, but it isn't going to work for me. I am confused. I'm afraid I won't get enough support here in Los Angeles. I am serious about getting free in this lifetime. I was wondering if I could have a private appointment with you to discuss this. I will come see you at your convenience.*
>
> *Love,*
> *Jan Banaszek*

A few weeks later, I received a brief note in response.

> *Dear Jan,*
>
> *We received your note. At this time, Kali will not be meeting with anyone privately, except those on the serious path.*
>
> *Maria*

My heart dropped.

Who the hell is Maria? And why didn't Kali answer me personally? I AM serious, and I have been nothing but loyal to the group from the beginning.

As I grappled with feeling discouraged, hurt, and confused, I was comforted by an inner voice.

"Remember, Jan, no matter what happens, I'm here for you."

Eventually, the Angels of God Center moved to Colorado. Cathy followed, but I learned that Kali publicly declared that gay people could not be on the serious path or do the Intensive, and as Jose was gay, he was merely "allowed" to continue on the path, but in a limited way.

Maybe I didn't need it at that point, but hearing that gave me one more reason to question the entire movement.

21

⁂

LIFE AFTER "THE CULT"

*L*ONGING FOR THE DEEP SLEEP I EXPERIENCED AT THE
Intensive, and missing the camaraderie of my roommates, I began to have disturbing dreams.

One night I woke up abruptly from a nightmare where
people were running in front of me. I was trying to catch up
with them, but my legs were powerless and I was running out
of energy. I tried to scream for help, but no noise came out of
my mouth. Everyone else seemed to know where they were
going as I fell down and people rushed past me. Then I saw
someone in the distance with a lantern in his hand. He was
walking toward me, and I trusted him.

As I drifted away from my involvement with Angels of
God, I slowly realized that I felt different about myself. I had
more compassion for myself and for others; I felt more em-
powered and I was listening to myself more. I was determined to
break through, with or without a master. I had God.

But even though I was stronger than ever, it was difficult
to completely let go. I still believed, as I did when I was a
good Catholic girl, that Angels of God was the only way
home. I feared that if I didn't follow this path, I would be

lost—or in Catholic terms, go to hell. I didn't want to risk that, so I held on.

But I couldn't deny that not everything Kali said made sense to me. How could she say that gays could not become free? How could she ban them from doing the Intensive and be so hypocritical? I simply could not go along with that. Yes, the organization had taught me a great deal about love, God, and myself, and I knew those gifts would last me a lifetime, but Kali's perspective and my future involvement with the group just didn't feel right anymore.

Since Christine and my family had been warning me for some time about the group, I began researching cults. I read books written by journalists and by people who became deeply immersed in the inner circle and escaped. Searching the Internet, I found a site warning about destructive cults. The light went on: Angels of God fit the description of a cult to a tee.

Angels of God had one leader who claimed to be the voice of God.

Angels of God said it was the only way home.

Angels of God targeted people with money.

And, as bizarre icing on the cake, Angels of God had a recovery group online.

The site was exactly the kind I'd been warned about at the retreats, when we were also told not to talk to anyone about what was going on, especially the press (and we were discouraged from reading bad press if we ever came across any). My discerning mind immediately took over. I knew people who posted on the site were angry and that it was personal, but I also couldn't deny that I had witnessed some of the things members of the recovery group were talking about.

I had been in the room when Kali told people what to do and where to go. I heard her tell one couple to get a divorce.

Like with Jose, Cathy, and me, she told others to move to new cities, right away, without question. She advised couples to have babies to bring in the next generation of followers.

Of course everyone had a choice. But there was an element of fear in that room—fear that if you didn't do what Kali asked, you would lose your path to freedom. And, perhaps worse, lose your connection with God.

As one last hurrah (if you could call it that), I decided to go to the Angels of God annual retreat, only because I longed to be in touch with the people I'd fallen in love with before. I still relished the sense of community and connection I felt with those people, and I wanted that feeling back.

At one point during one of the meditations, someone started chanting Kali's name. People began walking in single file around the room until almost everyone was slithering like a large snake, chanting Kali's name.

I started to follow, but I stopped and thought, *What am I doing here? Who are these people?*

A lot of them were intelligent, professional people I admired. But watching them blindly follow Kali as if she were God was disturbing. There was too much focus on her, and she wasn't even there—she was supposedly in Hawaii praying for us. On the recovery site I'd found, several people had speculated that Kali and others were involved in abusing narcotics. I couldn't help but wonder if that was true.

At one of the gatherings, there was an opportunity to ask questions of Helen, the leader of the retreat that day who spoke on behalf of Kali. She didn't look like Kali, but if I closed my eyes, she sounded just like her. It was as if Helen was channeling her.

I wasn't one to make waves, but I needed to ask a question that had been nagging me and my hand flew up in the air. Someone rushed over to me with a microphone and I held it in my trembling hands. Feedback from the microphone squealed in all our ears for a moment as if to stifle what I was about to say.

"I was wondering," I said tentatively, "why has Kali banned gay people? I don't understand. Aren't we supposed to be inclusive?"

The room fell silent.

Helen hesitated for a moment, then she reacted coldly. "Kali is the voice of God and this is what she has decided, so there's no need to question it. It's policy."

"But—"

"Jan, let's not waste any more time on this. If you don't agree, then you can leave."

The woman kneeling beside me reached out for the microphone, and I handed it back, dumbfounded.

I scanned the room, trying to find someone who felt as I did, someone who was no longer convinced, but all I saw was a sea of expressionless faces that all looked the same.

I knew then that I was done.

After returning from the retreat, I continued researching cults and reading the recovery blogs from people who had left. This helped me in my quest to carry on without the group, as I struggled to acclimate to life without the support of the other "Angels."

IT WAS YEARS LATER THAT TERI CALLED ONE DAY WITH news. She hadn't gotten as involved in Angels of God as I had, but she'd just received an email saying that Kali had died and she wondered if I knew.

"What?" I said wide-eyed. "What happened?"

Teri didn't know any details, so I went online and discovered an article that said Kali had died of liver failure, and it was speculated that it was likely due to substance abuse. The Angels of God site stated she'd died as her husband did: "... because the energy of God was too much for her body."

Oh please, I thought, rolling my eyes.

Ironically, I realized how addicted I had remained through the years to the idea that Angels of God and Kali were the only way for me to be "free." I thought I had abandoned that notion long ago, but it had lingered in my consciousness like the guilt and shame from my childhood, and the idea that the Catholic Church was the only way. But that day, upon learning about Kali, I finally felt the lift of disconnection from the cult.

Teri and I discussed our relief that we were no longer connected with Angels of God. We had continued our Actualism meditations and appreciated the contrast—Actualism was calming and centering, and although it was more cult-like when we originally started, after the founder died, it became a more democratic organization, far from the Angels of God environment.

One thing I had learned was to keep my connection with God intimate. So I began to write heartfelt letters to Him, asking questions in the way I would ask a trusted and intimate friend. The amazing part is that I would automatically, without conscious effort, feel called to write back to myself. And blessedly, the answers came easily.

Dear God,
Please help me. You gave me the Intensive and a group of
people to get free with, and now it is being ripped away.
How can I survive without this lifeline, God? I tried to
move to San Diego, but it felt wrong, and yet I don't want
to give up my pursuit of the truth, my freedom. Where do I
go from here, God? Please show me the way.
Love, Jan

My Dear Beloved Jan,
I am always here for you. I am not abandoning you. It is
good for you to let go of this group now and move on in
your life. Remember, the most important thing is to follow
your inner pull, even when the ones familiar to you are
going in a different direction. Keep going, my sweet one.
Love, God

I had heard these words before and taken comfort in their familiarity and the sense of intimacy they brought me. As my life was opening up through writing the letters, the love I was learning to feel for myself expanded to include everyone, and I began to allow and accept that each person's path was different, that there wasn't necessarily only one path home.

With God becoming a real part of my life, there was nowhere left to go but inside, where everything was happening. Through daily experience I was learning that I do indeed create my own reality, that God is my partner and always with me. Before, I had wanted to simply surrender and let God do it all, but now my role was becoming clearer to me.

As I continued my quest, spiraling even more intensely into a search for enlightenment that would last in my life, I met a woman at work who was a Buddhist. She invited me to a meeting where everyone was chanting Nam Myoho Renge Kyo. At first, I was a little put off and wondered if it, too, was a cult, but it felt good to me so I trusted it.

They told me that it was okay to chant for what I wanted, that I deserved it, and they talked about the "mystic law." Though I didn't fully understand it in a logical sense, it gave me a sense of peace inside that I had experienced in Actualism and other types of meditation. They taught me that by chanting Nam Myoho Renge Kyo, I could tune into my true nature and be connected with the source of all that is. A big concept,

I know, but it felt good and so I continued to chant with the group on a weekly basis and on my own.

After several months of chanting every day, I received my Gohonson, which is a beautiful symbol of the state of Buddhahood, intended to invoke the Buddha within. This was incredibly enlightening to me as I realized God, Buddha, was within me. I chanted for peace of mind. I chanted to find my soul mate. I chanted, trusting that what came to me was for my highest good and the highest good of all concerned. And I continued with my Actualism practice.

The one area of my life, however, that still felt unsettled to me was intimacy. Though I longed for a normal relationship with a man, I was still negatively affected by my relationship with my father. I loved him, but I continued to feel the need to push him away for fear of him getting too close physically. He never developed healthy boundaries, and he still emanated the fantasy of being "God's gift to all women." Not only did I find that arrogance annoying, but it was difficult not to project my father's inappropriate behavior onto other men. For that reason, I consistenly felt awkward with physical closeness, even though I desperately desired it.

Alongside my uneasiness with intimacy resided my fear that I would not be able to be myself in a committed relationship, that I might lose all that I had gained during my time of being single and finding God to be my "main squeeze." I didn't want to have to compromise the person I was for someone else, and after my first marriage so long ago, I knew I wanted it to be different the next time. What I didn't know was how I would explore a new way of sharing my life with another person.

A NEW BEGINNING

ONE AFTERNOON IN 2001, TERI CALLED AND ASKED
me to meet her for a drink after work. Relaxing with
her that night, we talked about Actualism, which we had now
been practicing for over twenty years. The key, as we both
knew, was to find our strength from within, not from without, like a guru or cult.

The annual Actualism retreat was approaching, and Teri
invited me to go with her. Every year, students would come
together to meditate and mingle, and it was an opportunity to
be with like-minded people and to experience the power and
love we felt in coming together as a group. It was being held
at a retreat center near the beach, and a getaway sounded
nice.

I had not gone to one of these retreats in years, and after
the Angels of God experience, I was hesitant to attend. But
then I reflected on how my Actualism sessions had always
taken me to a deep place within, and I realized that it was this
place inside of me that I needed to reconnect with. I remembered learning how to free up the flow of energy in my body.
I was longing for the inner harmony that my teachers had
spoken of, the relationship between my own magnetic and

dynamic, masculine and feminine—what they called the inner marriage.

So Teri and I went to the retreat together. And despite the fact that I didn't know the other attendees well, I felt at home for the first time in a while.

WAYNE

*W*ITH NO DESIRE TO BE HURT OR ABANDONED again, I had decided it was better to keep God as my partner—after spending so much time searching for the perfect man, I reasoned I couldn't lose with God at my side. Still, I chanted to find my soul mate. And as I began to feel stronger, I started to believe I could be in a relationship without losing myself.

A few months after the retreat, I received a call from Teri. "Do you remember a woman named Nancy at the retreat?" she asked.

Initially drawing a blank, I said I wasn't sure.

"She goes every year. She's close to our age, dark curly hair, pretty. She came without her husband. Remember we saw her crying at dinner on Saturday night?"

I recalled her then. I hadn't spoken directly to her, but I did remember being fascinated with her. She had come to a session wrapped in a blanket, clutching it around her as if for protection. I was drawn to her sweet and open face. Her hair was curly and loose, and she looked like she had just gotten up from a nap and hadn't had time to worry about how she looked, nor was she even aware of her physical appearance, a freedom I appreciated.

I had opened my eyes several times during one of the meditations and noticed that Nancy seemed illumined by a strange, magical energy that pulled me in. I wondered what her story was, what the connection was I had felt to her. She had a sad quality about her, coupled with beauty and vulnerability.

"I do remember her," I said. "She was really pretty and mysterious. What about her?"

Teri paused. "She killed herself."

"What?"

"I know. It's so sad. Do you want the details about the funeral?" Teri asked. "I'm going."

"Oh," I said. "Well, I didn't really know her ... so I guess not."

Teri understood. But for days after our conversation, the vision of the mysterious woman in the blanket stayed with me.

THE FOLLOWING YEAR, TERI AND I ATTENDED THE ANNUAL retreat together again.

As Nancy had come alone the previous year, I had not met her husband. But this time, Wayne was there. He was a quiet man, big and burly with gray hair and a moustache. I felt sorry for him, having lost his wife by suicide only months before, and I imagined he was likely still reeling from the loss. The group was sensitive to his pain, and to Nancy's absence, and he received a lot of attention. Every time Nancy was mentioned, his eyes welled up with tears. He would look around the room in gratitude, occasionally putting his head in his hands.

I felt for the heavy burden he was carrying, wondering what was behind his sad, deep brown eyes, thinking how brave he was to be there. As I watched him hug people with the big bear hugs only that kind of man can give, I wondered what I could do to help him. Though I was afraid of saying or doing the wrong thing, I felt a desire to comfort him without getting too close.

At dinner on Saturday night, one of the men lifted his glass and toasted Wayne as "the most eligible bachelor in the group." I thought it awfully soon after his wife's death to make such a declaration, but it was obvious that some of the women were interested in him.

I, however, wasn't one of them. I wanted an available man who could take care of himself and me, not one whose emotions I would have to babysit. I was certain he would find a woman willing to be there for him in his grief; I had my own issues to worry about. But at the same time, I found myself wondering what it would be like to be held by him.

Jan, don't go down this road again.

THE FOLLOWING AFTERNOON, TERI AND I PUT ON OUR bathing suits and headed for the hot tub. Wayne and a man named Robert were already there, and after I eased into the swirling warmth, Robert took one look at me and frowned. "You look tense," he said. "Come over here, and I'll massage your neck."

Hmmm.

My whole body was tense, and the idea of a neck massage sounded great.

Why not?

I liked Robert's zest for life and that he kept his body in shape. Though he was a bit older than I was, he had the sparkling eyes and energy of a much younger man—the type I wanted to end up with. He came on a little strong for my taste, but I scooted closer to him, and he turned me around and began rubbing my neck and back. His hands made their way around my body, landing on pressure points that immediately relaxed me.

I noticed Wayne quietly observing and wondered what he was thinking.

Then Robert's hands moved down a little too low, and though his touch was firm but gentle, I didn't trust him. When his hands wandered down to my butt, I tensed up.

Who does this guy think he is?

"I know how to make women relax," he said. "I find those pressure points that help them let go. Just relax, float, and trust."

He pressed on my sacrum with the fingers of one hand, sending a soothing wave of relaxation through my hips.

"See? Like that," he said. "Nothing to be afraid of."

With a smile of satisfaction on his face, he maneuvered me into an upright position and moved on to Teri. She relaxed into his touch, but I noticed that she, too, gently pushed him away when his moves became uncomfortable for her.

Wayne continued to silently observe as he checked Teri out, and I assumed he had an interest in her. By the time we left the hot tub, I was convinced there was a spark between them.

ON SUNDAY AFTERNOON, AS WE WERE GETTING READY TO leave, Teri mentioned that Wayne had come looking for me to say good-bye. Flattered, I welcomed his hug when he found me and lovingly hugged him back.

"Okay if I call you sometime?" He whispered in my ear.

"Sure," I said.

I was used to men asking for my number and then never

calling, so I didn't expect to hear from him. Yet I reasoned that maybe he would call—and actually hoped he would. I didn't give him my number and he didn't ask for it. But it was on the contact list, so I knew he could easily find me.

Weeks passed, then months.

I tried to shake the memory of his hug, the safe feeling it gave me, but I couldn't. It remained for weeks and somehow felt like a part of me, like it was warming me from inside.

Then one day I came home to a message on my answering machine.

"Hi, Jan. This is Wayne. Just calling to see how you're doing. I'll try calling you again."

It wasn't much of a message, but he did call again, and when I heard his voice, my heart skipped a beat or two.

"Oh ... Hi, Wayne," I said, trying to sound nonchalant.

"I tried to call you several times after the retreat," he said, "but the phone just kept ringing. Then I realized I had an old phone list. I finally got your new number."

I wasn't sure I believed that, but I had indeed changed my number awhile back.

"So, are you going to the Maui Retreat?" Wayne asked.

At the prior event, we had both expressed an interest in attending a trip to Maui that was being organized by one of the Actualism teachers.

"I think so ... but the airfares are so high. Do you have your ticket?"

"I do."

I hesitated. "How much was it?"

"Too much, but I wanted to get it early."

I liked that he sounded like a man who knew what he wanted, and he didn't seem too concerned about the price. He wasn't sweeping me off my feet, but I wasn't anxious to hang up either. Feeling spurts of energy shooting up and down my body, I wondered if there was something worthwhile there. I giggled to fill in the uncomfortable silences, but after awhile we both ran out of things to talk about, and the silence weighed heavily on the line.

"Well, it was good talking to you, Jan," he finally said. "I'd like to call you again if that's okay."

"Sure," I said. "I'd like that."

But I was conditioned to disappointment and felt that old anger coming up again, at all the men who had let me down. I questioned whether he would call again, and I was a bit annoyed that he didn't ask me out on a date, but I purchased my ticket for Hawaii anyway and was looking forward to the trip.

ABOUT TWO WEEKS BEFORE THE HAWAII RETREAT, Wayne left me a voicemail.

"Uh, hi, Jan, this is Wayne." He spoke slowly and calmly. "I'm leaving for Glacier National Park tomorrow. I'm meeting Nancy's adult daughter, brother, and some of our friends to spread Nancy's ashes and have a memorial ceremony for her. Glacier was one of her favorite places. I'll be back a few days before the Maui retreat and will call you. I'm really looking forward to seeing you there."

My heart leapt and I smiled, delighted that he thought enough of me to share such personal details. I felt both giddy and moved as I replayed the message a few times, touched by Wayne's devotion to his wife, even after her death.

I waited until the next day to call, when I knew he would be on his way to Glacier. After giving careful consideration to what I was going to say, I wrote it down and rehearsed it multiple times. Without sounding too intimate, I did want to convey how deeply he had touched my heart with his message.

Though I was prepared to talk if he picked up the phone, I

hoped he wouldn't. So when I heard the comforting beep, I read what I had written, doing my best to come across as relaxed and unrehearsed.

"Hi Wayne. Thank you for letting me know what's going on in your life. I want you to know that you have my love and support, and that I'll be thinking of you and Nancy and your family this week. I'll be there in spirit. Okay, talk to you soon."

No matter where this was leading, I was already feeling a special bond with this man and an undeniable connection with Nancy. I knew that her essence would be there with us, and I didn't have a problem with that. My heart was opening to the wonder and excitement of a new friendship ... and maybe more.

WHEN HE RETURNED FROM GLACIER, WAYNE CALLED TO tell me he was back in town.

"So, how was it?" I asked.

Silence.

I realized then that I had no idea what he was feeling, of how emotional the trip may have been for him.

But then Wayne's voice filled the uncomfortable gap.

"I met Nancy's daughter and brother at the airport, and then we stayed in a lodge that Nancy and I used to stay in. We got up early the next morning and met up with some friends who live near there. We began our hike to Grinnell Glacier, where Nancy and I hiked a few years ago with a group of friends." Then his voice broke. "For me, each step was a memory of my life with Nancy. I can tell you more when I see you."

"I'd like that," I said, hoping he could hear the compassion in my voice.

Then he added, "I wrote a poem about the experience, and I'd like to share it with you sometime."

Oh my God, who is this man?

"I would love to hear your poem, Wayne. Thank you for thinking of sharing it with me."

Our conversation then turned to the Maui trip.

"Don't worry about a car at the retreat," he said. "I'm renting one, and you can ride around with me."

"Okay. Thanks," I said, marveling at how considerate he was. Then I added, "I'm really concerned about the mosquitoes. They like me, and I'm afraid I'll get bitten. The first time I went to Hawaii I got bit on the lip, and it swelled up. I was uncomfortable being around people and it ruined my trip."

I rolled my eyes, glad he couldn't see me. *Why did you tell him that, Jan?*

"I have plenty of mosquito repellent," he said with a chuckle. "I'll bring some for you. I won't let those mosquitoes get near you. But I can understand their attraction."

Caught off guard by his teasing, I managed a giggle, followed by a long silence. I filled the pause with the thought that he was too good, that something must be wrong with him. But the truth was, I could have stayed up all night on the phone with him.

"Well, I guess I'll see you at the retreat," I said.

"Okay, see you there."

I relished the tingling sensation swirling through my body, but I didn't know what it was like to be in a solid relationship with a man, and though Wayne seemed honest and trustworthy, the fact that his wife had died by suicide suggested he might have a dark side.

What am I getting myself into? I wondered.

My heart was beginning to open and it was scary. I could tell that Wayne was capable of commitment, intimacy, and long-term love; it was obvious he loved his wife very much, even now while he was moving on. And he had kept his word to me. He called when he had said he was going to call.

While my conditioning warned me to push him away, my intuition said he was safe.

I would find out which was true soon enough.

24

❦

PARADISE

*W*AYNE'S ENERGY LINGERED IN ME AND I WAS
filled with anticipation of what could be next in
my life. It was 2002 and I was nearly fifty-five.

The sun was high in the sky when the plane landed at the
Maui airport in Kahului on a cheery Saturday. A couple I
knew from Actualism classes were on my flight, and we rode
together to the middle of the rainforest where the retreat was
being held at a yoga site. When I arrived, my mind was reeling from the sea of familiar and unfamiliar faces alike and the
bare-bones accommodations.

Feeling out of place, I allowed a guide to show me to my
room—my name was taped to the door, along with another name
I didn't recognize, and I wondered if I had just arrived at summer
camp when I saw the three sets of bunk beds and a large loft.

Where's my suite with room service and private bath?

"I thought I was getting my own room," I complained. "I
didn't want a roommate."

But the guide had already disappeared. Just then a trim
young woman who looked to be about eighteen stepped quietly down the ladder from the loft in her bathing suit and said
a quick "Hi."

I cringed as she headed outside, embarrassed that I had

dared complain when someone could have been in the room. Alone in the "dorm," I consoled myself with the thought that it was larger than what I'd shared with four of my sisters growing up, and that I only had to share it with one person. Plus I had my choice of six beds, top or bottom bunks.

Maybe it's not so bad after all. I'm in Hawaii!

Armed with suntan lotion and mosquito repellent, I went outside to explore. In the outdoor dining area, I met up with a few people who had just arrived and together we walked a trail beyond the lodge that wandered into the rainforest.

As reality set in that I was on vacation, I shook off my reservations about the mosquitoes and drank in the sounds of the birds chirping merrily and the smells of the forest that awakened my senses, welcoming me to paradise.

I wondered when Wayne would arrive.

After walking up the path and finding a swimming pool that seemed to melt into the mist of the rainforest, rain began to stream down. Deciding to make the most of it, we took off our shoes and jumped into the water. The air was warm and moist and the rain poured as if it would never stop. I luxuriated in the warmth of the water and in the sensation of raindrops bouncing off my face.

Noticing the edge of a slide that seemed to wind back into the woods and end in the warm pool, one of the guys got out and followed the narrow path up and around to find its origin. A few minutes later the forest rang out with a steady scream punctuated by bursts of laughter as he slid into the pool with a whoosh.

Eager to try it myself, I hiked up the way he had gone and found the top of the slide tucked away in some bushes, as if it hadn't been used in years. It was far away from the pool and I was scared. I considered backtracking, but I didn't want to look like a fool.

It's just a slide, I told myself. *But how fast will I go? Will I be out of control? I could get hurt, or even drown.*

And then I heard that trustworthy, inner voice.

"Jan, it's only a slide. Just get on and let go."

Embracing my brave side, I carefully climbed onto it.

"Time to let go, Jan!"

I was alone, but I heard those encouraging words loud and clear.

The surface was as slippery as grease, and after I let go, I quickly picked up momentum, winding out of control. As the turns in the slide rushed me head-on into the unknown, with bushes on either side and no certainty that this was the slide that led to the pool, excitement and fear collided into freedom, and I heard a combination of screams and laughter coming out of me. It was exhilarating and unpredictable, like falling in love, never knowing where it's going to take you next.

When I hit the water, the others cheered and clapped as I floated toward the surface, almost as if I had just entered the world as a brand new person.

BY DINNERTIME, EVERYONE HAD ARRIVED BUT WAYNE. As a small group of about twelve people, including some children, we felt like we were a family, which was how I used to feel with my Angels of God friends.

But where was Wayne? Did he decide not to come? *Maybe he changed his mind,* I thought. *Well, that's okay. Now I can relax.*

At least that's what I tried to convince myself.

But just as we were getting ready to leave for our rooms for the night, he walked onto the patio.

"I'm here!" Wayne announced, opening his arms.

People got up to greet him, taking turns embracing him.

"How did you find us in the dark?" someone asked.

"It must have been everybody's energy that guided me here," he said. "Thanks for lighting my way."

Nervous, and wondering what kind of relationship we were moving toward, I was one of the last ones to walk up and hug him. When I commented on how much I liked the lei he was wearing, he took it off and placed it around my neck. We both laughed, and I looked down as the blood rushed to my face.

We met as a group the next day to plan some activities. We would gather to meditate in the mornings and evenings, and our days would be filled with the magic of Maui.

I snuggled into a bottom bunk that night, eager to experience the island. My roommate, who kept mostly to herself but was delightful and fun, slept in the loft.

After meditation and breakfast in the common area the next morning, we teamed up in a few cars with plans to meet at a snorkeling beach. When Wayne invited me to ride with him, I scrambled into the front seat beside him before the two other single women even had a chance.

As I wondered if they were interested in him too, I looked over at Wayne's hands. They were big and strong, and I wondered what it would be like to wrap mine in his. When we finally arrived at the beach, I noted that his strong, well-shaped legs complemented his muscular arms, and there was no denying the attraction between us. It was the same energy I had felt before with him, but it had grown more real. I found myself longing to be held by him, wondering if he felt the same way.

Wayne invited me to get up early the next morning with him to catch the sunrise at Haleakala. But after accepting the invitation without hesitation, my mind began to play tricks on me.

Four o'clock in the morning is really early.

It might be raining.
I'm in unfamiliar territory.
Wayne might not show up.
He may decide to sleep in.
I don't want to be disappointed.
I don't know if I want to get up that early.
Then, finally, *Oh hell, why not?*

At precisely four o'clock the next morning, Wayne knocked gently at my door so as not to disturb my roommate. Still dark and pouring rain, it seemed like the middle of the night. I wondered what in the world we were thinking.

But it didn't take long to discover that we weren't the only sunrise enthusiasts. Cynthia, one of my Actualism teachers, approached us outside with her new boyfriend Hank to ask if they could ride with us. Hank was a New Yorker with crazy hair and an animated personality, and he was like a little kid discovering life for the first time. Overflowing with energy that burst forth in quick opinions and witty comments, he inspired me to lighten up and enjoy the moment.

We arrived at the crater with about a half hour to spare before sunrise. As Wayne helped me out of the car, he gently put a blanket around me to keep me warm. I wasn't sure whether it was the cold or the feelings he was stirring up in me that set my body to shaking and made my stomach jittery.

A crowd was gathering as a glow began to emanate from the horizon, cutting the dampness in the air, which vibrated with an aura of expectation as we waited for this awe-inspiring daily event to fill our senses.

Wayne and I chose a spot on a rock, and after I sat down with him behind me, he put his arms around me. Still shivering inside, but with warm, tingly waves of energy shooting through me, my breathing began to deepen until it was in unison with Wayne's. As I melted into him, content to be in the moment with this man, brightness expanded throughout the sky and lit up the crater.

I giggled happily and squeezed Wayne's warm hand. When his hand squeezed back, it was as if we had been together before, and this was our reunion.

After that memorable morning, we began to act like a couple while on the retreat—and people treated us that way. Wayne would walk me to my room every night and wake me up in the mornings, wearing only his pajama bottoms, knocking gently and popping his head in to say good morning. When I arrived for breakfast, I would walk directly into his welcoming arms. When dinnertime came, he would wait for me to show up so he could sit with me. Needless to say, he was slowly winning my heart.

For one of our outings, we hired some locals to take us up to the sacred pools in Jeeps. The guides showed us places they said the average tourist would never see, giving us a thorough history of the island. At one point, they took us to an area nearly devoid of other people, where we jumped into the sacred waters and swam through slow-moving pools until we came to a waterfall. Surrounded by the water's energy, I felt a deep sense of connection. But as I watched people climb onto one of the higher rocks to jump into the cold, clear water, I recognized this as another challenge for me to face.

I flashed back to swimming lessons at the local pool when I was six. Terrified of jumping, I stood there frozen in fear. Now, after climbing up and gazing down into the water, I felt that same fear.

"Trust me, Jan. You are safe," I heard within myself.

At that moment, I jumped. With my body electric with the freedom of choosing to trust, I swam toward Wayne, who received me lovingly, acknowledging how difficult it was for me to let go.

SITTING ON A BENCH OUTSIDE THE LODGE THAT NIGHT waiting to go to dinner with friends, I leaned my head against Wayne's chest as if it belonged there. He placed a soft kiss on the top of my head—a magical kiss whose energy was somehow familiar to me. I realized that the energy was overflowing from within me and returning to me, uncontained. It was at that moment that I wondered if Wayne was the one.

Although I had asked that question many times before, this time it came from a place of inner knowing. I was clear that no one person could meet all my needs, and I was certain that my relationship with God would be included in any relationship I chose to move forward with. But when I looked into Wayne's eyes, I saw the reflection mirrored back to me that I had sought for so long. The fleeting experiences I'd had with other men were replaced with a feeling that was solid, with an image that was real. It was I. It was God. There was no separation. I saw God in Wayne's eyes, looking back at me.

THE NIGHT BEFORE WE LEFT, I SAT ACROSS FROM WAYNE in the hot tub. As he gave me a knowing nod, his eyes watering slightly, I understood he was conveying that something was definitely happening between us.

Just then, Cynthia and Hank splashed in, laughing and kissing and openly caressing each other like teenagers spending the night away from their parents. I moved closer to Wayne, longing to be more playful with him, but he didn't respond.

Am I missing something? I wondered.

When Hank and Cynthia departed to continue their playful antics elsewhere, Wayne looked at me.

"Are you dating anyone?" he asked.

"No," I said. "Are you?"

"Yes ... I am."

My heart dropped. I was already more attached than I wanted to be. If he was still mourning his wife, that was one thing. But being unavailable because he was dating someone else was something altogether different.

He read the confusion and disappointment in my eyes. "But I'm planning to break it off with her when I get back."

I glanced away, then back at him. "Well, let me know what happens. I don't want to date you if you're dating someone else."

I was proud of my conviction; I knew what I wanted and I wasn't about to compromise. But I also couldn't slow my heart down or ignore my strong feelings for him. In the end, I decided I would continue to enjoy what little time we had left together, hopeful he was telling me the truth about calling off his present relationship.

As we sat with our arms around each other in the airport, waiting for our respective flights, Wayne drew my attention to an affectionate couple sitting across from us, and then to other couples who had moved closer to one another in the last few minutes.

"See what we started?" he grinned.

Basking in that loving feeling, I tried not to think about how I might never hear from him again.

2 5

⁓

AFTERGLOW

*W*HEN I STEPPED INTO THE OFFICE MONDAY morning, I was aglow with that something mystical that had touched me in Maui—and I knew it was more than the typical infatuation I had experienced in the past.

I was in love.

That next morning I received an email from Wayne.

Hi Jan. I broke up with that woman I was dating. I hope you still want to see me, because I would love to see you again.
Love, Wayne

I had returned from Hawaii a new woman in ways I was just beginning to recognize, and now, the man I thought might be just a vacation fling hadn't gone away. I had to take the risk. I couldn't think of any reason to stop myself from following my heart and getting to know this man better.

But I knew it wasn't going to be easy.

The specter of Nancy was still in the picture, and Wayne didn't try to hide his bereavement. They had been seeing a therapist together, and Wayne had continued even when

Nancy refused to go with him. I considered it a good sign that he was dealing with his grief by seeing a professional, and I did want to know more about the circumstances surrounding Nancy's passing. In the coming days, Wayne decided to open up to me, and I embraced the rawness he was willing to reveal.

When Nancy's mother died, she fell into a serious state of melancholy. Around the same time, she was suffering from a severe form of temporomandibular joint dysfunction (TMJ) and had gone to numerous doctors and dentists, seeking relief from her pain to no avail. After being diagnosed with depression, she bounced from therapist to therapist, refusing to take antidepressants. Wayne said he had tried to help her, but that he felt frustrated and helpless in the face of her changing moods and the growing gulf between them.

"Toward the end," he said, "when I realized there was no way I could reach her, I just tried not to rock the boat too much. I walked on eggshells, doing my best to make her happy."

As I listened, I wondered when Nancy had reached the point where she felt she could no longer go on, and I felt myself judging why Wayne couldn't have done something more. But when he told me that he believed Nancy must have lost perspective when she couldn't relieve the pain, and that her depression masked unhealed emotional pain from the past, I couldn't help but feel empathy for them both.

In her last semester of college, Nancy discovered she was pregnant by a man she didn't want to marry. She kept it a secret, even from her family, and then she moved to California. When it was time for the baby to be born, she called a cab to take her to the hospital, where she delivered a baby girl she relinquished for adoption.

Nancy never had any other children, and at forty, she married Wayne. Then, years later, Nancy received a call from the daughter she had given up, who was named Julia. Now grown, she was in her mid-twenties and had apparently been searching for Nancy for quite some time. Nancy was delighted to hear from her, as she too had been hoping to someday reunite with the daughter she gave up. Nancy and Julia found they had much in common and Wayne said they greatly enjoyed their times together.

It seemed Nancy had found some degree of joy again; she had been in a better mood, and he was relieved that things were on the upswing. So when Wayne returned home one night after officiating at a high school football game, he was surprised when Nancy was nowhere to be seen.

Calling out her name, he climbed the stairs and noticed that the door to the guest bedroom was closed, which was unusual. Sensing that something was wrong, he entered and found that the adjoining bathroom door was also closed. He walked slowly toward it, the droning noise of the fan magnifying the tension in the air.

"Nancy, are you in there?" he called out, praying she would answer as he eased the door open.

On the other side, he found Nancy's lifeless body in the bathtub. Just a few hours earlier, she had been sitting on the couch reading a book; he had kissed her and gone off to the football game. Now she was dead. How could that be?

He realized there had been some warning signs—she had told him several times after her mother died that she felt suicidal, but she had reassured him by saying that she would never kill herself because she was fearful of the physical pain.

He had believed her.

Reaching down to touch her arm, he recoiled as he felt its cold limpness. In her blood-soaked hand dangled his moustache scissors. On the floor was an empty bottle of pain pills—pills she was prescribed for the TMJ but hadn't been taking because she didn't believe in prescription drugs. Her open eyes were vacant and faded, no longer the deep brown windows to the soul he had known so well.

He immediately thought that she couldn't possibly be dead, that there must be something he could do. But it was too late.

"Oh my God," he repeated over and over. When he dialed 911, it was all he could do to gasp, "She killed herself."

And then the barrage of questions hit him: "Who are you? Where are you? Are there any guns in the house? Don't hang up ... officers are on the way."

When the first policemen arrived, their voices seemed distant and vacant. They told him the room was a crime scene and asked to be led upstairs. As police and paramedics inspected the house thoroughly, one officer brought Wayne downstairs to talk to the chaplain, who arrived soon after.

"Who can you call to be here to support you?" the chaplain asked.

Wayne drew a blank. No one came to mind. Finally, he thought to call Mario, his buddy and fellow football official with whom he had just had dinner. Mario came right over, his only comfort in a haze of disbelief and pain.

WHEN WAYNE ASKED ME OUT THE NEXT SATURDAY, I couldn't make it because I was expected at an afternoon party, which happened to be in Whittier, the same area where Wayne lived. I couldn't stop thinking about him while I was there, and I also thought that being so close to his house would be a good opportunity to see where he lived. That would tell me a lot about him, I reasoned.

Having made my appearance at the party, I decided to call Wayne.

"Oh, hi! How are you?" he said, sounding happy to hear from me.

When I told him I was in Whittier, he said, "I'd love to get together with you. There's a restaurant near here with a band that plays good dance music. Would you like to go dancing?"

"Sure!" *Wow! A man with a plan. That's a turn-on. And he likes to dance.*

"Would you like to come to my house?" he asked. "We can go from here, or ..." he hesitated a moment. "Or we could meet there, at the restaurant. Whichever is most comfortable for you. But I'd love for you to come here."

My hesitation was short-lived. "Okay. I'll come there."

As I drove toward his house, I pictured him living in a rustic older home on a tree-lined street. My stomach fluttered with excitement as I drove through several "bedroom communities" to an area that was lined with small houses. He had told me he lived in a gated community, and as I approached the gate in the pre-twilight, I saw a secluded community of a couple dozen modern two-story houses with children playing in the street.

So far, so good.

I called Wayne from my cell phone to let him know I had arrived, and he ran down the block to let me in. Then he opened my passenger door and got in to guide me to one of the biggest houses in the neighborhood, set back on a corner away from the others.

The house was beautiful. Multi-level with white walls, high ceilings, and interesting architecture, it was decorated in pastels with a feminine aura. I noted the pictures of Wayne and Nancy, some including her daughter, scattered throughout the house, wondering if he was indeed ready to move on with someone new.

He showed me around, and then an unaccustomed awkwardness overtook us. We weren't in Maui anymore. We were in Whittier, California, in the home he had shared with his wife.

"So are you ready to go dancing?" Wayne finally asked.

But I was no longer as interested in dancing as I was in spending a quiet evening getting to know each other better. So, I suggested we watch a movie at home instead.

We rented *Defending Your Life*, a film centered in "Judgment City," a place where people go to review their lives after they die. As we watched it, I was reminded of that place inside of myself willing to push through my fears to get what I wanted. And of course I was face to face with one of my biggest fears that evening: the possibility of being in a committed relationship.

As I rested my head comfortably on Wayne's chest during the movie, I at once felt the usual sparks of new love with the feeling I had known him for a long time. When the film ended, I stood up slowly and told him I should probably get going.

"Are you sure?" he asked, rising to put his arms around me and pulling me gently toward him.

"Well, I should," I said. Then I looked up at him and stood on my tiptoes, following my impulse to kiss him as he leaned down toward me.

It was a dreamy kiss, and he was so gentle, so loving and caring, that I wanted to simply melt into him and stay.

"You're welcome to stay here," he invited. "It's late, and you have a long way to drive. You can sleep on the couch, or you can sleep with me. I promise I'll be a gentleman."

I was pretty sure I could trust him, but could I trust myself? I had faltered in this area before.

Wayne's calm voice interrupted my inner conflict, repeating his invitation and his assurances. Clear about my boundaries, and believing I could indeed trust him, I accepted his invitation while the voice in the back of my head protested.

It's too soon.
What if I break down and have sex with him?
This isn't right.
I need to be careful.

But I had spent a week with this man in Hawaii without surpassing my bounds. I could do it here as well.

I agreed to stay with him in the master bedroom, but when we lay down beside each other in his king-size bed, I couldn't help but think that this was the bed he had shared with Nancy. But despite keeping myself covered, as did he, I couldn't stay away from him. It was like I had found home lying in his arms, and sleep was impossible. All night long I felt restless inside as I moved around, hugging him and then sitting up, keeping my awareness clear. Energy shot back and forth between us like laser beams. But although I reveled in the anticipation of making love with Wayne, I knew I needed to take things slowly.

"This is moving fast," I said in the darkness.

"I know," he said.

He was saying all the right words, but did he really know what he was getting himself into?

Did I?

26

CONSUMMATION

AFTER DATING FOR A FEW MONTHS AND HONORING my promise to myself not to move forward too quickly with Wayne, I felt ready for our relationship to advance to a more intimate level. Not willing to take any chances, however, I insisted we both get an AIDS test. Wayne agreed, and lucky for both of us, we each tested negative.

It had felt more like years, not months, that we had waited to be together completely, and the anticipation of it was almost more than we could bear. So after fixing him dinner, sharing some wine, and watching a movie, it was no surprise that we fell into a deep kiss—and that our clothes quickly found their way to the floor as we made our way into my room. Our passion for each other consumed us as we made love, as our inhibitions melted away in each other's arms.

"You do understand, Wayne," I said, stroking his chest, "that this kind of relationship isn't going to be a bed of roses. I mean, when our dysfunctions begin to collide and our issues come up to be healed ..."

"I know," he said, not sounding worried.

But suddenly, *I* was worried. Merely mentioning the words "dysfunctions" and "issues" put fear into me. I wanted to believe him as I looked into his deep brown eyes and heard the reassuring tone of his sexy voice, yet in the back of my mind I still questioned whether he had what it would take to break through the ingrained illusions that had manifested in our past relationships. Not only that, but I had worked hard to move beyond my old ways of being, and I knew that I would have to get out if it was not taking me in the direction of healing.

OVER TIME—PERHAPS INEVITABLY—REALITY INDEED SET in, and as the butterflies of new love fluttered a little less frequently, life began to chip away at our dream of the perfect relationship. But instead of jumping to the conclusion that it wouldn't work out, I was prepared to face whatever challenges we had; getting real about our life together simply meant that it was time to take a look at whether the good we created together outweighed the bad. I realized I was projecting onto him my feelings from the past with men who didn't treat me well or abandoned me, and while I knew he didn't deserve my anger, it was still oozing out in ways I knew would have to be contained, or better—healed.

And there was Nancy. The truth was that throughout the first phase of our relationship, she continued to impact our life together. She showed up in Wayne's dreams, encouraging him, he said, to journal, giving him the message that he needed to move forward. While this was helpful to Wayne, it also wasn't particularly easy; those emotional ties couldn't simply be cut.

Nancy and Wayne had belonged to a running club that not only did local runs, but also traveled together all over the world. Striving to ease himself into our new bond while holding onto his past, Wayne asked me to join him for a gathering with some of his friends from the club. Wanting to support him, I conceded to hanging out with a bunch of strangers, but every time I went, I felt left out. The group called each other weird names like "Bull" and "Shit" and they always ended at a bar, where they proceeded to drink and indulge in sarcastic humor. I had never understood the fun of sarcasm—it left me feeling uncomfortable. And I was concerned about the focus on drinking, considering my family history.

To me, it didn't seem like these people respected Wayne or understood him, and even though I knew Wayne wanted me to fit in with the group and continue on like he and Nancy did, I just couldn't do it. I fought with myself on it and made an attempt to go along with it, but when I realized that I needed to follow my inner guidance, I simply stopped going. Wayne continued to spend time with them, which I knew I couldn't stop, but I decided it was not going to be a deal-breaker for me. I admit it was a relief, though, when the meetings tapered off after awhile until he stopped hanging out with the old clan altogether.

It was then that Wayne and I found more things we enjoyed doing together. We not only liked the same kinds of movies and TV shows, but we also went hiking and bike riding, relishing outdoor activities in each other's company. What's more, we gave one another the space to do things with other people. Not wanting to lose the bond with my girlfriends, I continued to hang out regularly with them, but it was sometimes at the expense of being with Wayne during a crucial time in our relationship. I should have realized that my true friends would understand our spending less time together, but I was still holding on to what was familiar, in case things didn't work out between Wayne and me.

Over time, Wayne slowly let go of Nancy—and I let go of what I perceived was my need to be free.

Without my realizing it, I discovered that I had a delicious freedom in our relationship—and that with a supportive man like Wayne by my side, I could actually be freer than I imagined possible. Only it wasn't quite so easy for me to shed my past conditioning.

OUR NEXT BIG HURDLE CAME AFTER WE HAD BEEN DATING for six months. After traveling back and forth between Whittier and Hollywood, about an hour's drive or more, Wayne expressed a desire to sell his house so he could find a place closer to me. Although we had considered moving in together, we had come up with all kinds of reasons why that wouldn't work for us, mostly because we felt it was too soon. To help us decide if living together was indeed a good next step for us, Wayne suggested we both talk with his therapist to see what ideas she might have.

"So why don't you two look for a place together," she suggested, "and see how it goes?"

But when we brought up our reasons why we thought it was a bad idea, they no longer seemed to make sense—and it was hard to hide behind our excuses in front of an objective third party.

"Perhaps before you do this," the therapist said, "I think you ought to have a symbol of your commitment. A promise ring perhaps, or an engagement ring."

Whoa, I thought. *Am I ready for this? To commit myself to this man for the rest of my life? To get married?*

We had talked about it, of course. We were passionate about each other and about the relationship, and it seemed we were definitely headed in that direction. So with some degree of reticence, we agreed to start looking at houses.

But despite my excitement about what could lie ahead for

us, I remained apprehensive about commitment, afraid that inside of me—under wraps but still very much alive—raged an anger no relationship with a man, not even Wayne, could soothe.

27

⌘

SURRENDER

*F*OR THE PAST SEVERAL MONTHS, I HAD BEEN ATTEND-
ing a women's group one Saturday a month, not too far
from where Wayne lived. Teri was also in the group, and
it became our tradition to go out to dinner together afterwards. After our dinners, I would usually head to Wayne's
house for the rest of the weekend.

One Saturday, not long after our session with the therapist, Wayne asked me to have dinner with him. He had apparently forgotten about my monthly women's group, which
was meeting that day, so I told him I'd join him for a drink
near his place after our gathering and my regular dinner with
Teri.

Teri and I got caught up in girl talk, and I ran a bit late to
meet Wayne, but since we were only having drinks, I wasn't
too worried. I was looking forward to being with him as I
drove to his house, assuming we would be going to one of our
usual restaurants close by. When I arrived, I was surprised to
see Wayne in slacks and a nice shirt. I was dressed much more
casually in jeans, but he didn't seem to mind so off we went.

Without saying much, Wayne ushered me to his car and
drove the two blocks to our favorite Italian restaurant. When

I asked why we were going there, given that I wasn't dressed accordingly and he gave me no heads up, he dismissed my question with a casual wave of his hand.

The host took us to a table in the back, and we ordered glasses of wine. I was surprised that Wayne hadn't eaten since he knew I had gone to dinner with Teri, but he said he wanted to wait and eat at the restaurant, so he ordered dinner as I sipped my wine. He seemed quite nervous and didn't eat as heartily as he normally did. Then he got up and walked to the front of the restaurant. When he returned a few minutes later, I asked him what he was doing.

"Who me?" he said coyly. "I just wanted to order dessert for my birthday."

"Your birthday?" I said. "That was last week. We already celebrated." I sat back and squinted. "What are you doing?"

A few minutes later, the waitress arrived with tiramisu. "On the house," she said.

She placed it in front of me, and as I was about to pass it across the table, I noticed an unmistakable sparkle on the top.

Wayne sat across from me, grinning from ear to ear as the waitress stood there smiling, then quietly disappeared.

Hardly daring to breathe, I felt with my fingers for what I knew must be a ring. When I pulled it out, it was covered with cream so I stuck it in my water glass. When I pulled it out, I saw the diamond.

"Oh my God," I said in a quiet voice, looking up at Wayne.

"Jan," he said, "I love you with all my heart. I want to spend the rest of my life with you. Will you marry me?"

My heart pounded at a crazy rate as I sat there speechless.

"I was going to kneel down and say it," he said.

"Okay," I said, relieved at the delay.

Wayne got down on one knee beside me and repeated the

words. "Jan, I love you with all my heart. I want to spend the rest of my life with you. Will you marry me?"

It was all happening so fast, while at the same time it seemed perfect. I had waited so long for this moment, and now it was happening. My husband had finally shown up.

"Yes," I said, beaming, allowing my heart to answer without my mind interrupting.

When it was clear I had said yes, the cheers began to echo around us. Wayne had come in earlier to plan it, so the wait staff all knew about the surprise.

As I reveled in the moment, however, the cheers became eclipsed with doubts. Striving to push them down, Wayne's faults began to magnify in my consciousness. As the bad tried to outweigh the good in my mind, all I could think through my reserved smile was, *Am I making a big mistake?*

But another part of my mind was speaking to me with authority, my own authority.

"This is what's real for you right now, Jan. Follow your heart. Everything else will fall into place."

Will it? I wondered skeptically. But then I reminded myself: *Maybe this guy isn't perfect. But he's perfect for me. Let's keep that clear and in perspective.*

WE SPENT MONTHS IN SEARCH OF THE RIGHT HOUSE—WE could have hunted into the next millennium, because "the right house" simply didn't exist for me. The housing market was highly inflated, and buyers swarmed the available houses and overbid on fixer-uppers, some of which weren't worth fixing up.

Having sold his house in a heartbeat at a good profit, Wayne was ready to move. But I was having trouble letting go of my comfortable little Hollywood apartment where I clung to the familiarity of my past.

Then, the right house appeared.

I knew it was a good house for us and Wayne fell in love with it instantly. We had only an hour to make a decision, though. If we didn't take it then, it would be gone.

After a glass of wine at a nearby restaurant, I realized that this was the moment of truth. The house was nicer than anything we had seen—it wasn't a fixer-upper, and it was empty and ready to move into. Yes, it was more money than we had planned to spend, but that was to be expected in this market, and Wayne was sure we could handle it.

"Jan, this is the best house yet. It's in a nice neighborhood. It's clean. It doesn't need work. I like it. And I need to move now."

But what if I'm not ready? I thought.

But I couldn't say it. It didn't make sense.

Wayne was right. This was a good house, and we could do it.

Though I couldn't think of a logical reason to say no, I sat there, silent, for what seemed like hours until at last I whispered, "Okay."

NOW THAT WE WERE ENGAGED AND BUYING A HOUSE together, marriage was of course the next logical step. But I was not about to take that leap until I was absolutely sure Wayne was the man for me. I was counting on us living together for the answer to that question.

Contrary to the feedback I'd received while pursuing previous relationships, the people who mattered to me in my life believed that Wayne was good for me. No one was warning me to stay away as in the past, and everybody was in agreement that it was safe for me to move forward with him. Although I knew it was most important that I feel secure within myself, it was wonderful to finally witness my loved ones accept my man with no doubts.

Always my voice of reason (though I had often ignored it), Christine was completely supportive of my relationship with Wayne. When she met him, I didn't experience the usual tension I had felt with previous boyfriends; in fact, I felt a warmth between them, as though they shared a common interest in wanting what was best for me. Sure, she had a few concerns at first, but they came from a place of caring. Overall, she accepted him, and us, as a couple.

Despite the overwhelming support I had from my circle, I returned to therapy to help me sort through my significant life changes; I also worked with an acupuncturist who helped me listen to my body through muscle-testing. Using this method, I started revealing past traumas that were coming up to be healed—to clear the space for my new love. I learned that my body often reacted automatically—which meant negatively—to the relationships from my past. Now it was time to surrender to the love inside of me being reflected out to the world.

Looking back, I had come a long way from the innocent, confused girl who easily gave her power over to others, particularly men. In my heart, I knew I was finally ready to live in a healthy partnership with a man.

With God.

With Wayne.

But my inner child was still wounded and needed soothing, so I began listening to a CD of sweet lullabies called *Songs for the Inner Child*. As I drifted off to sleep each night, Shaina Noll's soft, nurturing voice reminded me of that place inside where I knew I was loved unconditionally— that same place I remembered as a child, where the voice resided that had always been with me, as close as my breath.

It had taken a lifetime to discover, but I finally realized that the sweet, supportive voice had been my own, that higher place within me I had been calling God was so close, so intimate, so profoundly me. It was all coming together for me—what God was for me in my life. In Actualism it was explained as the Higher, coordinated with IE (Incarnating Ego), as equal partners. It was me and it was God, and we were one voice.

DURING THAT TIME, SOMETHING SHIFTED INSIDE OF ME. I can't say exactly when, but I felt like a current was carrying me and that it would take more energy to go against it than to surrender.

Years before, when I was single, I went on a road trip by myself and discovered a magical place off Pacific Coast Highway called Ragged Point. I can remember standing on the grass between the sheer cliffs above the ocean and the majestic mountains, as a wedding took place in a gazebo at the edge of the cliff. I prayed then, as I had before, to find my soul mate. Though I'm still not sure what a soul mate is exactly, I know it's not the same as the ideal I once had in my head. It's something tangible and lasting. And Wayne was the only person I had ever shared this special space with.

Now, immersed in a true relationship, that magical place above the Pacific Ocean began to call to me ... and I was listening.

"Let's get married at Ragged Point," I said to Wayne.

"That sounds perfect," he said, taking me in his arms.

After calling Mom and my sister Lynn, I called Christine. After all we had been through together, I was overjoyed to tell her that I had found what I was searching for all those years. I had not only found myself, but I was ready to commit to a good man—for keeps. She'd seen me through so many failed relationships and heartaches, and now I wanted her to share in my joy. Undeniably thrilled for me, Christine gave me her blessing in support of our union.

ON AUGUST 5, 2006, MY ENTIRE FAMILY SHOWED UP TO witness this magical day in my life. I didn't think they'd all make it to the location we'd chosen, but somehow, they each arrived.

Wayne and I recited our vows to each other in front of God, our families, friends, and, I like to believe, a host of angels—during the service, a cluster of dragonflies fluttered around the gazebo and over the audience.

I was 58 years old.

I continue to move forward in this adventure with my loving husband, and in my inclusive love affair with God, always staying in touch with that supportive and ever-present inner voice. The brilliant diamond on my finger is a constant reminder of my commitment to God, to Wayne, and to the sparkle within myself to stay focused on the light that is always there, guiding me gently into the mystery.

EPILOGUE

$\mathcal{M}$Y HAND SHOT UP.
Something was different. I was different. I had
raised my hand before, but not without a lot of shaking and
trepidation. Now, however, I was confident.

When one of the teachers in the front of the room called
on me, I stood up and she handed me a microphone. I wasn't
sure what I was going to say, but it didn't matter. I was as
comfortable as if I were standing in front of my best friend. I
put the microphone close to my mouth.

"Hi. I'm Jan."

I looked around the room and I could see and feel every
person in the room, all 250 of them. It was the last session of
the weekend, a gratitude sharing. I had a lot to be grateful for,
and a sweet and profound energy enveloped me.

After almost two years of facing my truth—in the presence of these people in a graduate program at the University
of Santa Monica that I began in 2011—I felt like I had returned home. I was no longer the person who held back and
hid, blushing when noticed. That woman filled old shoes. I
had new shoes on now.

I was grounded solidly in my body. And I was present.

I had experienced a similar feeling before, in the breakthrough Intensive I attended in 1994. The feeling was an energy

that had been ignited from deep within—an all-encompassing, calming, and yet unbelievably exhilarating and exciting feeling.

At the Intensive, I was aware of the other people in the room. They were all in their own individual processes, and I was feeling a deep compassion for all of them and for myself. I understood their suffering in a way I never had before, while feeling a sense of peace in myself.

But since that time, the realities of my life had shadowed my peaceful energy. I kept sinking into a place that was familiar to me, burdened by the unfinished business of my past. I was aware of the freedom of letting go, but there was a force that continued to pull me down.

Call it illusion. Call it resistance. Call it the devil. Call it what you like. I felt as if I was living in two worlds, pulled apart inside.

After leaving the familiarity of the Intensive group, I set an intention to focus on my relationship with God. I wondered what it would be like if I lived in a place of acceptance, integrity, and creativity. Why not have a relationship with God? I reasoned. One with all the ups and downs that accompany a real relationship?

Thus, as my relationship with God developed, I came to understand that a love affair with God was really a love affair with myself. It was that realization that sparked my writing, and in 1998, I began documenting my story.

By the time I completed the first draft of this book, I was in a loving relationship with Wayne, my now husband. I attributed our healthy and perfectly timed relationship to my newfound love and respect for myself.

While I was unwilling to settle, strong in my convictions, I still felt incomplete. A deep yearning remained in me, a longing to be my authentic self in the world, using the gifts I knew I had been given. I was feeling unfulfilled in my position as a legal secretary in a large downtown law firm, and I felt a deep desperation to share my story.

My therapist suggested graduate school as a possible next step for me, and I was referred to the University of Santa Monica (USM). When I explored the website, I was intrigued but cautious. Perhaps jaded by the barrage of spiritual possibilities available, as well as all my past experiences, I wasn't sure I wanted to put more money into the "promise of freedom."

The Intensive group had promised I could break free from the illusion in this lifetime. USM, on the other hand, offered what appeared to be a more down-to-earth and realistic path, that of "a Divine Being having a human experience," of moving up the "Soul Line" while moving toward the "Goal Line." What's more, they offered a graduate degree in something I had been studying for most of my adult life: *Me*.

USM called it *Spiritual Psychology*, which translated to confronting any obstacles that were keeping me from experiencing the Divine Being I knew I was. It would mean facing that pull inside of me whose job it was to keep me small. Originally, that pull was in place to protect me from harm, but now I was safe, and I believed I could turn this dividing force into an ally.

The first year at USM was a challenge, and by the beginning of the second year I thought I might drop out. However, despite my inner resistance and the pain I endured with all the program brought up for me, I recognized the opportunity as one for healing in a loving environment and ultimately decided to stay.

As my second-year project, I chose *Awakening to My Inner Artist*. This included completing my book and allowing my internal artist to be expressed through an Artist's Way course. In preparing for the creative process, the teacher asked us where in our bodies we were feeling the creative energy. For me, the undeniable movement was in my womb. Suddenly, I understood the meaning of the words in the Hail Mary, "Blessed is the fruit of thy womb."

Having recited this prayer over and over when I was a child, the words were familiar but the meaning had escaped me. Now I realized that just as Mary carried Jesus in her womb, or so the story goes in the Catholic tradition, I felt a movement, an energy, a tingling inside of me that was ready to be born into the world. I came to understand that this energy is always present, that it repeatedly resurrects itself because it comes from a place that is my source— the energy of God within me. It is available to me always, and it is the place from which I create. Through this realization, I discovered the true meaning of co-creation— that God is that close to me, inside of me at all times.

This was the energy that caused my hand to shoot up and take hold of the microphone.

As I stood poised to graduate in front of the group I had committed to being with once a month for two years, the words I wanted to say to my fellow students flowed easily:

> "I can feel each and every one of you in this room right now. I want to thank you so much for being here with me through every stage of my blossoming in these past two years. I honor myself for never giving up, and I am so grateful for this loving environment, which has allowed me to look at myself more deeply than ever before. Because I love myself, I can love you, and I can receive your love."

By the time I graduated from USM in 2012, I had completed several large pieces of art, one of which I showed in the school's art gallery. Another piece I was honored to feature on the cover of this book.

❦

DAD PASSED AWAY AT THE END OF 2013. HE WAS NINETY-three and in his own private world. In the end, he didn't always recognize who I was, and that made it easier for me to be with him. I would look into his eyes and see sweetness, love, and pain. I told him he hurt me and that I forgave him. He looked back at me in a vacant yet knowing way, and we gently completed our contract for this lifetime.

About two months after Dad died, Mom began slowing down. She had always been there for us—sitting by the second-story kitchen window watching the cars go in and out of the driveway, staying in touch with each one of us, whether we were in town or not. Each day at around 2:30 p.m., I would dial her number and hear her sweet voice say, "I'm listening ..." and I would reply "Hello, Dahling" in the old Hollywood style that was so dear to her.

All eleven of us siblings were in contact and doing our best to make it as easy for Mom as possible in the comfort of the home she and Dad lived in for fifty years, the home she found for us through her desire and her prayers.

One day, the social worker showed up to check on Mom. "Are you ready to get on the bus?" he asked. She knew what he meant and said yes.

The night she left, several of us were sitting around her bed telling stories of old times and laughing together, with Mom's favorite Frank Sinatra music playing in the background. In the middle of our laughter, my sister Tracie stopped us all and said, "I think this is it." At that moment, we profoundly and reverently witnessed her last breath.

I felt a deep connection that night with my brothers and

sisters as we let go of the physical presence of our beloved mother. No, she was not perfect, nor was she a saint. But she accepted and loved each one of us. She also held us together in a way that we needed to let go of in order for each of us to move on.

Over a year later, after a lot of grieving, each in our own way, along with differences yet to be healed, we collectively let go of the big brown house on the hill in Hollywood. We let go of what once was, each beginning anew.

ACKNOWLEDGMENTS

When I began this labor of love in 1998, I knew it was going to be a collaborative/co-creative project. I am grateful to all the angels who came forward in perfect timing to help me bring my story out into the world in the form in which it has evolved.

My first acknowledgment is to God, which to me means that part of me that sees the bigger picture and loves me no matter what.

I acknowledge those people who believed in me before I believed in myself and carried me until I found my wings, so to speak.

Thank you, Mary Anne, for giving me the unconditional love I needed to believe in myself and in my gift.

Thank you, Arthur Flowers, for acknowledging before I realized it myself, that I am a writer and I do have a voice.

Thank you, Arthur Mikaelian, for believing in me and for showing me a way through my insecurities and darkness into the Light of my soul, and what I am here to share and how to share it in a way that includes many different perspectives.

I honor the Goddesses of Crystal Vision (Sue, Anne, Debby, Vivian, and Elisabeth) for believing in me and for inspiring me to do whatever it took to keep going, trust myself, and manifest my story in its purest form.

Thank you, Stan, for always believing in me and helping me grow and evolve into who I am.

Thank you to Ellen, Nomi, Chiwah, Brenda, Molly, and Stephanie for your gentle guidance and editing and for showing up in the perfect timing.

Thank you to my fellow students at USM, who were there for me and believed in me when I was still struggling to believe in myself and my creation.

My special Circle group at USM (Katy, Rene, Afsaneh, and Gregory). Thank you for being so open and loving, and inspired, as I shared my story with you.

Thank you, Stacey, for your love and expertise and for being the one to help me refine my book and get it ready for publishing in its highest and best form.

And thank you, Wayne, for showing up and loving me as I was, as I am, and as I continue to evolve and grow in the crucible of our marriage.

ABOUT THE AUTHOR

JAN BANASZEK has been a lifelong explorer of mind, body, and spirit. A native Los Angeles resident and the third of eleven children, she left college to travel abroad, eventually returning home to marry her first love. After that marriage ended, she remained single for nearly thirty years, attending numerous workshops on personal growth to discover her authentic self. She found herself drawn to varied spiritual practices that helped her to connect with the Divine—Tai Chi, Actualism, Kundalini yoga, chanting (receiving her Gohono-son in 2002), and daily Vipassana meditation. After a spiritual awakening, Jan was encouraged to develop the journaling of her at-times tumultuous life into a book. She obtained a Masters in Spiritual Psychology at the University of Santa Monica, California, which not only resulted in completing *Gathering the Fragments of Myself*, but also in awakening her inner artist.

After a twenty-six-year career as a legal secretary, Jan is now retired and enjoying life with her husband, Wayne.

CPSIA information can be obtained
at www.ICGtesting.com
Printed in the USA
LVOW11s2352190517
535221LV00001B/229/P